Guardians of the Gateway: M Cisco's IDS/IPS for Unbreakable Network Security

Table of Contents

- ○ Early integration of IDS/IPS

- ○ Built like a tank, acted like a chameleon in network defense

- ○ The "vintage" option for small to medium enterprises

Chapter 4: Cisco Firepower 1000 Series – "The Newbie That Can"

- Advanced threat protection with a friendly price tag

- Quick deployment and simple management (It's like your first car: easy to handle)

- Key Features:

  - ○ Integrated next-gen firewall

  - ○ Multi-layered security, because one layer isn't enough

  - ○ User-friendly interface with a hidden beast inside

Chapter 5: Cisco Firepower 2100 Series – *Leveling Up* the Security Game

- Powerful hardware designed for the enterprise crowd

- Seamless security features: VPN, IPS, and NGFW all in one

- What makes it a game-changer in the IPS world

- "Does it break a sweat?" - No, but it makes your network sweat less

Chapter 6: Cisco Firepower 4100 Series – The 'Big Brother' in the Room

- High throughput and scalability: *If your network is a wild party, this is the bouncer*

- Advanced threat intelligence integration

- Hardware & Software combo for large enterprises: Think "bodyguard meets strategist"

- Features to make you feel like a network security guru:

  - ○ Flexible interfaces

  - ○ Cloud-ready defense

Chapter 7: Cisco Firepower 9300 Series – Welcome to the Big Leagues

- The big gun in Cisco's security arsenal

- Hyper-scalable security for massive networks (think: data centers)

- Why this is the device to have when you want to flex your security muscle

- What makes it shine:

    o Multi-Gbps throughput

    o Redundant and fault-tolerant architecture

    o Customizable and future-proof

Chapter 8: Understanding Cisco's "Firepower" – Is It a Mythical Creature?

- Diving into Firepower Management Center (FMC)

- How to manage multiple Cisco IPS/IDS devices from a single pane of glass

- User-centric dashboard (You can actually understand it, trust us)

- Real-time threat intelligence that feels like it's ahead of the curve

Chapter 9: Cisco Threat Intelligence Director – *More Than Just a Fancy Name*

- What's so 'intelligent' about Cisco Threat Intelligence?

- How the system adapts and learns in real-time

- Bulletproof your defenses with automatic updates and threat response

- Pro tip: Don't just sit back and relax—make the most of the automated features

Chapter 10: Integrating Cisco IDS/IPS with Other Security Solutions – Making Friends in High Places

- Cisco's role in the broader network security ecosystem

- How to seamlessly integrate Cisco IDS/IPS with firewalls, SIEMs, and other devices

- Why collaboration is the secret sauce in today's security landscape

- Practical guide to creating a seamless security environment

Chapter 11: From Setup to SNAFU: Configuring Cisco's IDS/IPS Without Losing Your Mind

- Step-by-step walkthrough: Configuration basics (No tears allowed)

- Common mistakes (Yes, we know you'll make them)

- Troubleshooting tips that won't make you wish you chose knitting

- Pro tips on avoiding "security overkill"

**Chapter 12: The Dark Art of Tuning Your Cisco IDS/IPS – *It's Like Finding the Sweet Spot on a Guitar* **

- Setting the right sensitivity (Yes, it matters!)

- Fine-tuning to avoid false positives (because no one wants a thousand emails)

- Balancing performance and security: The fine line of a cybersecurity maestro

Chapter 13: Real-World Scenarios: Putting Cisco's IDS/IPS to the Test

- Case studies: Real attacks stopped in their tracks

- How to recognize an attack before it even happens (and feel like a wizard)

- Tales of troubleshooting: Success and epic fails (It's OK, we've all been there)

**Chapter 14: Advanced Cisco IPS/IDS Features – *Is This Magic? No, It's Just Tech* **

- Advanced event correlation and analysis

- Integrating AI and machine learning: The future of IPS/IDS

- Automating responses to threats: Make your network fight back on its own

Chapter 15: Scaling Cisco IDS/IPS for the Big Fish – Enterprise-Ready Security

- Scaling Cisco Firepower across a global network

- Multi-location deployment without pulling your hair out

- How to ensure maximum uptime with redundant security solutions

**Chapter 16: The Future of Cisco IDS/IPS – *What Happens Next?* **

- Emerging threats and how Cisco's evolving to combat them

- The next big thing in network security: Artificial Intelligence & Automation

- Staying ahead of the curve in an ever-changing landscape

Appendix A: Hardware Compatibility Chart – Cisco Devices, from Legacy to Latest

- Quick reference guide to help you understand which hardware fits your needs

- From the old guard (PIX) to the new breed (Firepower 9300)

Foreword: Welcome to the Digital Fortress

Welcome, brave reader, to the realm of network security – a place where hackers lurk in the shadows, your firewall is your first line of defense, and *Cisco* is your trusty sword and shield. Think of this book as your roadmap through the perilous terrain of digital threats. It's not just a guide – it's your initiation into the mystical world of IDS and IPS, where *detection* and *prevention* are your battle strategies, and where you'll learn how to outwit the bad guys without even breaking a sweat.

In these pages, you'll embark on an adventure that spans the evolution of network security. We're starting with the humble beginnings of legacy Cisco hardware – those noble, but sometimes clunky, systems that paved the way for the advanced, sleek, and powerful tools that are available today. You'll get the lowdown on Cisco's most beloved devices, from the legendary PIX Firewall (bless its heart) to the modern-day powerhouse that is the Firepower 9300 Series, which could probably protect your entire network from a zombie apocalypse if you asked it nicely.

You'll find wit and humor sprinkled throughout (because who says securing a network can't be fun?), but also the expertise you need to understand the *why* behind the *how*. Because while it's tempting to just click "Next" until everything is magically configured, understanding the inner workings of your IDS/IPS devices is what separates the network security novices from the seasoned professionals. And don't worry – we're going to teach you to talk like an expert too, so that when your boss asks you why the system is still safe, you'll confidently respond with, "It's all about multi-layer defense, real-time threat intelligence, and a pinch of machine learning."

Inside these pages, you'll find step-by-step instructions, expert advice, and case studies that prove Cisco's IDS/IPS solutions are not only reliable but downright life-saving. This isn't just about the technology – it's about protecting your digital kingdom from the marauding hordes of cybercriminals out there who think they can just stroll into your network undetected. Spoiler alert: with Cisco on your side, they're in for a rude awakening.

So grab your coffee, boot up your Cisco devices, and get ready to unlock the secrets of network security. The fortress is waiting to be fortified, and you're the guardian. Welcome to the adventure – let's make your network unbreakable!

Chapter 1: Network Security 101 – Because You Need More Than Just a Password

1. **Welcome to the world of network security!** It's a big, scary place filled with threats, attacks, and the constant need to patch vulnerabilities. Now, before you rush off to change your password to "1234" (because it's *definitely* more secure than "password"), let's take a moment to appreciate the complexity of the digital world we live in. You see, when it comes to securing your network, passwords are just the tip of the iceberg. Sure, they help keep the door locked, but what happens when the burglars have a master key? Enter IDS and IPS – the real bodyguards of your network, standing guard 24/7, making sure no one sneaks in the back door. Passwords are like a sturdy lock, but IDS and IPS are the CCTV cameras, motion sensors, and alarm systems rolled into one. If you only rely on a password, you're basically leaving a neon sign above your network that says, "Hack me." Let's fix that.

2. **What is network security, really?** In a nutshell, it's the practice of protecting your network infrastructure from unauthorized access, misuse, or damage. You don't want random strangers poking around your data, right? Think of your network as a medieval castle, and you're the Lord or Lady of the domain. Your server? That's the treasure room. Your sensitive data? Priceless gems and gold. The bad guys? They're the invaders trying to breach your walls. But no one's going to break into *your* castle, right? Not if you've got the right tools, strategies, and a healthy understanding of how the bad guys operate. So, buckle up – it's time to learn the fundamentals of keeping your digital fortress safe from prying eyes.

3. **So, let's talk about passwords – and why they're not enough.** We've all been there: "Please create a password that's at least 12 characters, includes uppercase letters, lowercase letters, numbers, and at least one special character." The frustration is real. But let's face it – even if you've got a password that's a 128-character masterpiece of complexity, it's still just one layer of defense. Hackers know the tricks – they're counting on you to forget that *one* password hint you used for all your accounts. Also, don't even get us started on password reuse. It's like using the same key to open your front door, your car, and your safe deposit box. A password can be cracked. But when you add IDS and IPS to the mix? Now we're talking multi-layered security.

4. **Now, let's introduce IDS and IPS: The Dynamic Duo of Network Security.** If passwords are the lock on your door, IDS (Intrusion Detection System) and IPS (Intrusion Prevention System) are the watchful eyes that never blink. IDS is like a security guard who watches the perimeter, looking for any suspicious activity. IPS is the action hero – not only spotting threats but also slamming the door in their face before they can get through. Both are critical for modern network defense, and together, they provide a much-needed layer of protection against a wide variety of attacks. IDS might sound like the good cop – always monitoring, always alert. IPS is the bad cop – taking action, making arrests, and shutting down attacks in their tracks.

5. **What's the difference between IDS and IPS?** Think of IDS as the detective, always keeping an eye on everything, looking for signs of criminal activity. It spots suspicious behavior, raises an alarm, and notifies you. That's great, but it doesn't stop the crime from happening – just like a detective might tell you "Hey, someone's breaking into your house," but leaves it up to you to do something about it. IPS, on the other hand, is a superhero with a badge and a taser. It doesn't just report an intruder; it stops them in their tracks, actively blocking malicious activity as it's happening. So, while IDS is your trusty sidekick in identifying threats, IPS is the one making sure those threats don't get past your defenses. They work together – like Batman and Robin, but with more tech and fewer capes.

6. **The good news: You don't have to be a cybersecurity expert to use these tools.** Cisco's IDS/IPS solutions make it easier than ever to defend your network. You don't need to be able to recite the OSI model backward to get them up and running. While understanding the fundamentals is important, Cisco has streamlined the setup process to make security more accessible. After all, you've got better things to do – like binge-watching the latest show or pretending to understand the stock market. Let Cisco handle the heavy lifting of security while you focus on more important matters. But hey, if you want to dive into the nitty-gritty of network protocols, we'll happily take that journey with you, too.

7. **Let's talk threats – because, spoiler alert, they're everywhere.** Cybercriminals aren't just hanging out in basements anymore. They're sophisticated, organized, and they've got tools at their disposal that would make your head spin. From phishing attacks to ransomware, from SQL injections to Distributed Denial of Service (DDoS) attacks, the list goes on and on. Every time a new threat is discovered, it's like a cat-and-mouse game with the bad guys, who are constantly coming up with new ways to breach your defenses. IDS and IPS are your first line of defense against these digital villains, constantly scanning for signs of foul play. The goal is simple: stop them before they can get their grubby hands on your data.

8. **But what happens if you don't have IDS or IPS?** Oh, it's not pretty. Without these tools, your network is like a house with unlocked doors and windows, inviting thieves to waltz in and take whatever they want. Sure, you might have a basic firewall, but it's like putting a garden gnome in front of your front door and calling it a "security system." Hackers won't break a sweat. With IDS/IPS in place, you're not just adding an extra lock to the door – you're hiring a team of highly trained security experts who never sleep. And trust us, you want them on your team.

9. **How does IDS/IPS actually work?** At a high level, these systems work by monitoring traffic, analyzing patterns, and looking for anything that smells fishy. IDS examines inbound and outbound traffic, compares it to known attack signatures, and raises the alarm when it spots something suspicious. IPS does the same thing, but instead of just raising an alarm, it actively blocks malicious traffic. It's like having an automated bouncer who checks IDs at the door and throws out anyone who doesn't belong. Both

systems rely on databases of attack signatures, but the best ones also incorporate machine learning to recognize new and evolving threats.

10. **Let's talk about traffic analysis – because it's the bread and butter of IDS/IPS.** Your network is constantly humming with data – users browsing the web, sending emails, making transactions, and streaming videos of cats (because, priorities). But among all that normal traffic, there's always the chance that a little bit of malicious activity slips through. IDS and IPS constantly analyze network traffic to identify unusual patterns. Maybe someone's trying to send large amounts of data to an unrecognized external server? Or perhaps there's an unauthorized login attempt from an unfamiliar IP address? Both systems can detect these irregularities and respond accordingly – one with an alert, the other with a swift "Not on my watch!" attitude.

11. **Signature-based detection vs. anomaly-based detection – A showdown of styles.** Signature-based detection is like looking for fingerprints – it's searching for known patterns of malicious behavior that have been cataloged and stored in a database. It's reliable, fast, and effective against known threats. Anomaly-based detection, however, is more like a detective trying to figure out who's acting suspicious in a crowd. It looks for deviations from the norm, like unusual traffic spikes or odd behavior, and flags it as a potential threat. The beauty of Cisco's IDS/IPS solutions is that they blend both methods, providing both the speed of signature detection and the flexibility of anomaly detection.

12. **False positives – the necessary evil of IDS/IPS systems.** Let's face it: no system is perfect. Sometimes, IDS and IPS can get a little too excited and raise alarms for things that aren't really threats. This is called a "false positive" – and while it's frustrating, it's better than missing a real threat. You can think of false positives as the annoying but necessary alarm bell that rings every time someone sneezes. It's important to tune your IDS/IPS systems to reduce these false positives – kind of like teaching your security guard to stop calling the police every time a squirrel runs past. But remember, a few false alarms are a small price to pay for preventing a real attack.

13. **Why is network segmentation important?** Imagine you're hosting a huge party in your mansion, but instead of opening all the doors to everyone, you separate the rooms into VIP sections, regular guests, and staff. If someone sneaks into the staff area, they don't have access to your diamond collection. Network segmentation works the same way. By dividing your network into smaller, more manageable parts, you can contain a potential threat before it spreads. IDS and IPS help monitor traffic between these segments, ensuring that any suspicious activity is caught and dealt with swiftly, so the party can continue without interruption.

14. **Next-gen firewalls and IDS/IPS – Why you need both.** Firewalls have been around for decades, and they're still a crucial piece of your security puzzle. But as cyber threats have evolved, firewalls alone aren't enough. Next-gen firewalls (NGFWs) integrate many of the features of IDS and IPS, providing you with deeper packet inspection, application control, and threat intelligence. It's like having a bouncer who checks both the ID and the guest list. When you combine a next-gen firewall with Cisco's IDS/IPS systems, you're

creating a fortified perimeter with multiple layers of security. It's like building a moat around your castle, then putting up a drawbridge that only lets the good guys cross.

15. **The importance of updating your IDS/IPS signatures – Keeping your defenses sharp.** One of the keys to maintaining a strong security posture is keeping your threat database up-to-date. Hackers are constantly finding new ways to sneak in, and your IDS/IPS system needs to stay ahead of the game. That's why signature updates are so important. It's like getting the latest news on new cyber threats, so you can adjust your defenses accordingly. Fortunately, Cisco makes it easy to schedule updates automatically, so your system always has the freshest threat intelligence at its disposal. Because if you're not keeping up with the latest threats, you're basically leaving your front door wide open.

How IDS/IPS Affects Network Performance – Balancing Security and Speed.
When you add IDS/IPS to your network, it's like hiring extra security guards to watch every corner of your digital empire. But wait—more security means more scrutiny, and more scrutiny means more overhead, right? Well, yes and no. While it's true that having multiple layers of security can introduce some performance concerns, Cisco's IDS/IPS solutions are designed to minimize any impact on network speed. Think of it like adding extra lanes to a highway: More cars (data) can still get through, but now there's less chance of a traffic jam. The key is optimizing the configuration and using advanced features like traffic filtering, rate limiting, and load balancing to ensure your network remains fast while staying protected. Ultimately, the performance hit is minimal compared to the benefits of thwarting potential attacks. After all, what's the use of a fast network if it's full of holes?

Let's talk about updates – and why they're crucial.
Just like the software on your phone needs regular updates to protect you from the latest threats, so do your IDS/IPS systems. Updates are the lifeblood of your security tools. If you don't regularly update the signature database or the firmware, it's like leaving the front door of your house wide open while expecting no one to walk in. As we mentioned earlier, cybercriminals are always innovating, and without regular updates, your system becomes a sitting duck. Fortunately, Cisco's IDS/IPS devices come with automatic updates, so you don't need to babysit them. Think of it as the self-cleaning oven of security solutions—set it and forget it, knowing it's always up to date.

The human factor – Why your team is the weak link.
Ah yes, the ever-present weak link in the security chain: the human. You might have the most sophisticated IDS/IPS system, the strongest firewall, and the sharpest threat detection tools, but if your team is careless, it's like having a high-tech alarm system and then leaving your keys under the doormat. Employees clicking on phishing links, reusing passwords, or bypassing security protocols are the culprits. This is why cybersecurity training is just as important as your technical defenses. If your staff isn't aware of the latest phishing scams or doesn't understand the importance of network segmentation, even the best IDS/IPS tools can be rendered ineffective. Security isn't just about the hardware or software—it's about building a culture of security within your organization.

How IDS/IPS systems integrate into your larger security strategy.
Imagine your network security as a football team. The IDS and IPS are the defensive players—always on the lookout for attackers. But they don't work in isolation; they need support from other players like firewalls, SIEM systems, and threat intelligence feeds. A true multi-layered defense strategy combines all these elements, each working in concert to stop threats in their tracks. For instance, while IDS is detecting a potential threat, the firewall can stop it at the door, and a SIEM system can log the event for analysis and future prevention. The synergy between different security tools is what creates a truly resilient network, making sure that each layer covers the gaps of the one before it.

Incident response – The final frontier of security.
You've set up your IDS/IPS, configured your firewalls, and trained your team. But despite all that, breaches can still happen. And when they do, how you respond is crucial. This is where your incident response plan comes into play. It's like having a fire drill for when things go wrong. Your IDS/IPS will alert you to suspicious activity, but it's up to your team to act fast and decisively. You'll need to isolate the compromised systems, analyze the cause of the breach, and then take steps to prevent it from happening again. Having a solid incident response plan means you won't panic when the inevitable happens—and yes, it will happen at some point. With the right preparation and tools, however, you'll come out the other side stronger and more secure.

The role of machine learning in modern IDS/IPS systems.
In the past, network security was a lot like a game of whack-a-mole: You'd hit one threat, and another would pop up somewhere else. But with modern IDS/IPS solutions powered by machine learning, things are different. These systems are capable of learning from network traffic patterns, detecting new and evolving threats without needing constant updates. It's like having a security guard who not only monitors the door but also remembers the faces of everyone who's been in the building before. This allows your IDS/IPS to adapt and react to sophisticated threats that traditional signature-based detection might miss. While it's not a silver bullet (no security solution ever is), machine learning makes your defenses smarter, faster, and more effective over time.

The importance of compliance – Because hackers love loopholes.
If you think compliance standards like HIPAA, PCI-DSS, or GDPR are just boxes to check, think again. These regulations are designed to force organizations to think about security and implement the best practices. And while your IDS/IPS solutions may not *directly* ensure compliance, they play a big role in helping you stay on the right side of the law. For instance, using Cisco's IDS/IPS to monitor and block unauthorized access to sensitive data can help you meet requirements for data protection. Plus, they give you the peace of mind that you're actively preventing breaches—helping you avoid the costly fines and headaches that come with non-compliance. So yes, keeping your network secure might be about protecting your data, but it's also about avoiding the wrath of regulatory authorities.

Choosing the right Cisco IDS/IPS solution for your needs.
When selecting an IDS/IPS solution, one size does not fit all. Whether you're running a small business or managing a global enterprise, the right solution depends on the scale and complexity of your network. Cisco offers a wide range of options, from the compact Firepower 1000 Series

for small businesses to the powerful Firepower 9300 Series designed for large enterprises. If you're just starting out, a simpler, more cost-effective solution might be all you need. But if you're a major corporation with vast networks and complex requirements, it's worth investing in a high-end model. Cisco's offerings are designed to scale, so you can always start small and upgrade as your needs grow. The key is to choose a solution that balances performance, cost, and security features to match your specific use case.

What's next? The future of IDS/IPS technology.
The world of network security is constantly evolving, and IDS/IPS technology is no exception. As cyber threats become more sophisticated, IDS/IPS systems must also adapt, incorporating new technologies like artificial intelligence, behavioral analytics, and cloud-based solutions. In the future, we might see even more automated responses to security events, with AI-driven systems that can not only detect but also prevent attacks in real time. Additionally, with the rise of cloud computing and hybrid environments, IDS/IPS solutions will need to be more agile, offering seamless protection across both on-premises and cloud-based networks. The good news? Cisco is always innovating, ensuring that your IDS/IPS solution will continue to evolve and meet the ever-changing threat landscape. The future of network security is bright – and you'll be ready for whatever comes next.

In conclusion: You are now armed with the basics.
Congratulations! You've made it through the first chapter. You now understand the fundamental principles of network security, why passwords alone won't cut it, and how Cisco's IDS/IPS solutions can help you protect your network. You've also learned how these systems work, what threats they defend against, and why they're indispensable for any modern network. But this is just the beginning. The road to mastering IDS/IPS is long, but with the right tools, strategies, and a bit of humor along the way, you'll be well-equipped to safeguard your network like a true guardian of the gateway. Ready for the next chapter? Your network's security is about to get even stronger.

Chapter 2: Cisco – The Unsung Superhero of Network Security

1. **In the world of cybersecurity, Cisco is the quiet hero** — the one who doesn't crave the spotlight but has saved the day more times than you can count. While everyone's busy talking about the latest flashy gadgets and tools, Cisco is in the background, working tirelessly to ensure your network doesn't implode. Think of Cisco as the dependable but unassuming sidekick – never asking for credit but always there when you need them. But let's be real: without Cisco, your network security would be more "wild west" than "digital fortress." It's the unsung superhero of network security, using its gadgets and know-how to keep your data safe from bad actors. From firewalls to routers to IDS/IPS systems, Cisco's portfolio is nothing short of impressive. While other companies are still figuring out how to integrate their systems, Cisco's been seamlessly doing it for decades. And here's the kicker: They've been doing it with an unwavering focus on making security accessible, powerful, and — dare we say it — fun.

2. **So, what makes Cisco a superhero in the first place?**
   It's all about their comprehensive approach to security. Cisco isn't just about fancy hardware; it's about building an entire ecosystem that ties together firewalls, switches,

routers, and intrusion prevention systems into one cohesive, seamless unit. They don't just detect threats; they proactively stop them in their tracks, using next-gen firewalls and security appliances that integrate threat intelligence to safeguard your network from end to end. No one's trying to put out small fires here; Cisco is stopping forest fires before they even start. It's like having a superhero who can *sense* danger before it's even on the horizon. Their goal isn't just to react to threats; it's to predict and prevent them. Every product in the Cisco security family works in harmony, sharing threat intelligence, communicating with each other, and providing you with a fortress of protection. But let's not forget, they've also made it ridiculously easy to use—no need to hire a whole team of security experts just to deploy and manage their solutions.

3. **It all started with Cisco's foundation in networking.**
Before Cisco became the giant in network security, it was already a powerhouse in the world of routing and switching. Their networking hardware was so good, it practically defined the internet as we know it today. Cisco was essentially the backbone of early internet infrastructure, connecting networks worldwide with its robust routers and switches. That foundation gave Cisco an advantage in understanding the network like few others. With a deep knowledge of how data travels across the globe, Cisco was in the perfect position to build security tools that not only monitor the network but actively protect it. While many companies were focusing solely on data protection, Cisco understood that if you didn't protect the network *itself*, you were just putting a Band-Aid on a bullet wound. By leveraging its network expertise, Cisco was able to develop security systems that offer not just protection, but the intelligence to preemptively strike.

4. **Cisco's IDS/IPS: The Nighthawks of Network Security.**
If you've ever seen the movie *The Matrix*, you know the agents in the film are always a step ahead, seeing the future and acting before the threats even surface. Cisco's IDS/IPS systems work similarly, constantly scanning for potential threats and stopping them before they even get a chance to wreak havoc. The beauty of Cisco's approach is its ability to integrate into your network seamlessly, acting like a series of "nighthawks" who are always on the lookout. They don't just detect bad traffic; they analyze it, learn from it, and adapt to new attack strategies in real-time. And unlike those flashy superheroes who need a dramatic reveal before they swoop in to save the day, Cisco's systems work quietly behind the scenes. The best part? They keep getting smarter, learning from both current attacks and past data to stay ahead of cybercriminals.

5. **Why Cisco's integration is like a perfectly timed heist.**
Imagine pulling off a high-stakes heist. You need the best crew—everyone has a role, and each person works in perfect harmony to get the job done. That's how Cisco's security products function. Instead of having multiple, disconnected tools that you have to manage separately, Cisco offers integrated solutions where every device communicates with the other. Their security platforms don't just sit there and wait for problems; they share threat intelligence, analyze data, and block malicious activity across your entire network. It's like having a bunch of skilled professionals working together to keep your digital vault secure, all while making sure there's no room for error. The beauty of Cisco's ecosystem is that it provides a holistic security solution without all the hassle of managing each

piece separately. It's like orchestrating a symphony where every instrument is perfectly in tune—and no one has to stop to tune the strings.

6. **Cisco's Firewalls: Not Just Any Door Guards.**
   If you've ever watched a movie with a bouncer, you know the importance of a good doorman—someone who checks IDs, sizes you up, and makes sure the riffraff stays out. That's Cisco's firewall in a nutshell. But don't expect Cisco's firewall to just stand there and let anyone walk by with a fake ID. No, Cisco firewalls are like the bouncers at a VIP-only club, meticulously checking traffic for malicious activity before it even gets near your valuable data. They don't just look for one or two types of trouble; they use the power of deep packet inspection to analyze every single bit of incoming and outgoing traffic, checking for vulnerabilities, malware, or anything else that doesn't belong. The kicker? These firewalls are smart, flexible, and can be adapted to meet the needs of any size business, from the mom-and-pop shop to the massive multinational corporation.

7. **The Cisco Umbrella: A Cloud Security Shield That Keeps You Dry.**
   The cloud is often treated as the "wild west" of digital infrastructure: free-roaming and full of opportunity, but also full of potential dangers. That's where Cisco Umbrella comes in, offering a much-needed cloud security solution that ensures your network stays safe from the risks of cloud applications. It's like having an umbrella on a rainy day, but instead of keeping you dry, it keeps your data secure. Cisco Umbrella doesn't just monitor your traffic; it proactively blocks harmful websites, protects against malicious cloud services, and provides secure DNS layer protection to ensure you aren't walking into a storm without cover. Whether you're using cloud services for SaaS, IaaS, or anything else, Umbrella makes sure you're always protected.

8. **Not just hardware, but brains: Cisco's approach to security intelligence.**
   It's one thing to have the hardware to stop threats, but it's another to have the intelligence to predict them. Cisco has mastered both. Their security tools don't just sit idly by; they actively learn from network traffic, adapt to new attack vectors, and use threat intelligence feeds from across the globe to anticipate new threats. Think of it like training a super-sleuth who's seen every trick in the book. Cisco's security systems constantly evolve, adapting to new techniques used by cybercriminals, making sure that the moment a new threat emerges, they're ready to shut it down. By integrating Cisco's threat intelligence into your security systems, you essentially future-proof your defenses against attacks you haven't even seen yet.

9. **Why Cisco is a favorite of enterprises (hint: it's about scalability).**
   When it comes to securing large networks, scalability is king. Cisco has earned its reputation as a go-to provider for enterprises because their solutions can scale with the business. Whether you're a growing startup or a massive multinational corporation, Cisco's tools can handle the load. They've designed their security systems to grow with your needs, offering flexible solutions that can be easily expanded and adapted. And unlike some other security providers that throw you into the deep end with a sea of complicated settings, Cisco's platform makes scaling straightforward and efficient.

They're like the security equivalent of a Swiss Army knife – versatile and built to meet the ever-changing demands of the enterprise world.

10. **Cisco and automation: Because no one has time to babysit security.**
The world is moving at lightning speed, and the last thing any network administrator needs is to be glued to a monitor, manually sorting through endless security alerts. That's where automation comes in. Cisco's security solutions are built with automation at their core, allowing security teams to focus on high-level strategy while the system handles the mundane tasks. With features like automated threat detection, instant response, and intelligent reporting, Cisco's solutions ensure that your network is always secure without requiring a full-time security team to babysit it. It's like having a robotic assistant who never needs a lunch break and never forgets to respond to an alert. Because let's face it: Humans make mistakes, but automation doesn't need to check Twitter during a crisis.

11. **Cisco's Smart Licensing: When Licensing Doesn't Feel Like a Headache.**
Ah, licensing. If there's one thing that can turn a perfectly good day into a headache, it's dealing with licensing issues. Fortunately, Cisco's Smart Licensing makes the process smoother than a fresh jar of peanut butter. Instead of worrying about manual license renewals and tracking down key codes, Cisco's Smart Licensing system automates the process. It's like having a personal assistant who ensures you never forget to renew your security coverage, keeping your network fully protected at all times. Smart Licensing also gives you better visibility into what you're using and where, helping you make informed decisions about your security infrastructure. With this system, Cisco takes the guesswork out of licensing, so you can focus on protecting your network rather than managing paperwork.

12. **How Cisco Security Solutions Fit into a Modern, Hybrid Workforce.**
With the rise of remote work and hybrid environments, securing a network has become a whole new ballgame. But fear not! Cisco is always a step ahead. Their security solutions are designed to seamlessly integrate with both on-premises and cloud-based networks, ensuring that your employees, wherever they may be working from, are always protected. From secure VPN connections to cloud-based threat detection, Cisco ensures that whether you're in the office or working from a coffee shop, your network remains impervious to threats. Cisco's solutions ensure that the modern workforce can work without compromising security, making it possible to secure the perimeter while keeping things agile and flexible.

13. **Cisco's Security Platform: The Power of Integration.**
One of Cisco's greatest strengths lies in its ability to integrate. Unlike some providers that offer piecemeal solutions, Cisco's security portfolio works in harmony to give you a comprehensive defense. Every component, from routers to firewalls to IDS/IPS, is designed to communicate with one another, providing a unified view of your network's health. It's like having a superhero team where each member knows exactly what the other is doing. The benefit? A more efficient, effective security infrastructure that provides end-to-end protection. When all of Cisco's products are working together, they create an impenetrable fortress, designed to thwart threats no matter where they originate.

14. **Why Cisco is the security choice for the Fortune 500 (and you should consider it too).**

    Big corporations don't just choose Cisco because of its reputation; they choose it because of its unparalleled reliability, scalability, and security features. Cisco's products are trusted by the largest and most complex organizations around the world because they know that when it comes to securing a network, there's no room for compromise. And the best part? You don't need to be a Fortune 500 company to benefit from Cisco's tools. Whether you're a startup or an established enterprise, Cisco's solutions scale to meet your needs. So, when you're choosing your next security solution, remember: If it's good enough for the big leagues, it's probably good enough for you.

15. **The unsung hero: Why Cisco doesn't get the praise it deserves.**

    Despite being at the forefront of network security, Cisco often flies under the radar compared to other "sexier" security companies that love to tout their marketing jargon. But here's the truth: Cisco's strength lies in its consistency, reliability, and depth of expertise. While other companies may come and go, Cisco has been the backbone of network security for decades, quietly revolutionizing the way we protect data. They've always been the dependable, understated superhero that doesn't need a flashy cape. Instead, Cisco's legacy speaks for itself, providing robust solutions that stand the test of time. So next time someone asks you why Cisco is the go-to choice, just smile and say, "Because when you need security that works, Cisco's your hero—no questions asked."

Cisco's Reliability: The Rock-Solid Foundation You Can Count On.

When it comes to network security, reliability isn't just a nice-to-have feature—it's a must. After all, when your network is under attack, the last thing you want is for your security system to go down for a "scheduled maintenance" session or fail to perform under pressure. That's where Cisco really shines. For decades, they've built a reputation for creating systems that *just work*— consistently, securely, and without drama. Think of it like having a reliable friend who always shows up on time and never bails when you need them most. Cisco's products are trusted by thousands of organizations worldwide because they deliver high availability and minimal downtime. Whether you're using Cisco's Firepower devices, Umbrella, or any other security solution, they're designed to handle the toughest challenges without breaking a sweat. If you want peace of mind knowing your network is secure 24/7, Cisco's reliability is your best friend.

Cisco's Threat Intelligence: The "Future-Sight" Your Network Needs.

In a world where cyberattacks are constantly evolving, staying ahead of the game is essential. That's why Cisco's threat intelligence capabilities are so powerful—they're designed not only to detect attacks but to predict them. Imagine having a crystal ball that tells you when and where the next threat will strike, so you can preemptively block it before it even lands. Cisco uses real-time threat feeds from global sources, constantly updating its systems with the latest information on emerging threats. It's like a network security system that's always learning and improving. With Cisco, you get access to the most advanced, up-to-the-minute threat intelligence, ensuring you're always one step ahead of the hackers. The best part? Cisco's threat intelligence integrates seamlessly with its security systems, so when an emerging threat is identified, it can be blocked automatically across your network.

Security with Simplicity: Why Cisco Is the Antidote to Complexity.
In the world of network security, there's a *lot* of complexity. Between firewalls, threat detection, VPNs, and all the other components of a security architecture, it can be easy to feel overwhelmed. Fortunately, Cisco believes that security shouldn't be a maze of confusing options and impenetrable settings. Their goal has always been to simplify the process for network administrators while still offering powerful, enterprise-grade security solutions. Think of Cisco as the Zen master of cybersecurity: it offers solutions that are both deep and accessible. From user-friendly dashboards to intuitive setup wizards, Cisco has taken the guesswork out of network protection. Whether you're setting up an SMB security solution or managing a global enterprise, Cisco's security tools are designed to make your life easier, not harder. Simplifying security isn't just about convenience—it's about allowing you to focus on what matters most: keeping your network safe.

Cisco's Support and Community: The Superhero Sidekick You Didn't Know You Needed.
Even the best technology needs a little backup. That's where Cisco's legendary customer support and community come into play. Cisco's support system is like having a well-trained pit crew on standby, ready to fix any problem and get your system back up and running in no time. Need help with deployment? There's a support team for that. Got a bug or configuration issue? Cisco's support team is like a Swiss Army knife—ready to tackle any problem. Plus, Cisco has a massive, active user community, where you can find discussions, tips, and solutions to nearly every issue you might face. It's like being part of an exclusive club where everyone's goal is to make your network security stronger and more efficient. So, while Cisco's security products are top-tier, the support you get is what really makes them stand out. No superhero works alone, and Cisco's support team is there to help you along the way.

From Legacy to Cutting-Edge: Cisco's Evolution of Network Security.
While Cisco's security offerings are some of the most advanced tools on the market, they also have deep roots in legacy systems. Cisco has been around long enough to see network security evolve from simple firewalls to complex, AI-powered threat detection. As cyber threats became more sophisticated, Cisco didn't just rest on its laurels; it adapted and innovated, constantly pushing the envelope on what network security could do. Cisco's transition from legacy firewalls like the PIX series to the next-gen Firepower systems is a prime example of how they've embraced change without losing the core reliability that made them a security leader in the first place. It's like watching a classic hero evolve over time, refining their skills and abilities to meet new challenges. Whether you're dealing with old-school threats or facing the latest, most advanced cyberattacks, Cisco has the solution to meet the need.

Cisco's Vision: Securing the World, One Network at a Time.
The team at Cisco isn't just interested in securing individual networks—they want to create a safer, more secure digital world for everyone. Their vision is about bringing the benefits of advanced network security to all businesses, from the tiniest startup to the largest enterprise. Cisco understands that the digital landscape is constantly evolving, and they are committed to providing the tools that allow organizations to stay ahead of the curve. Their focus on security is driven by the idea that we need to work together to protect not just data, but the trust that underpins the entire digital ecosystem. Cisco's global reach and network of partners ensure that

security is built into the very fabric of modern networks. They're not just securing data—they're shaping the future of the internet, one secure connection at a time.

Cisco's "Security Everywhere" Philosophy: Defending from All Angles.

In the past, network security was focused mainly on defending the perimeter, with firewalls and intrusion prevention systems acting as the gatekeepers. But as the digital world became more complex—especially with the rise of cloud computing, IoT, and mobile devices—this "perimeter-only" approach just didn't cut it anymore. Cisco's "Security Everywhere" philosophy addresses this by integrating security across every part of the network. Whether it's protecting data on endpoints, securing traffic in the cloud, or safeguarding remote workers, Cisco's tools provide a comprehensive, unified defense. This approach ensures that no part of the network is left vulnerable, offering peace of mind no matter where your data goes. Cisco's security doesn't just stop at the network perimeter; it extends to every device, application, and user that interacts with your network. In a world where cyber threats can come from anywhere, Cisco's "Security Everywhere" approach is the ultimate defense strategy.

Why Cisco's Innovation Never Sleeps: The Future of Network Security.

One of Cisco's greatest strengths is its ability to innovate constantly. While other companies might rest on their laurels after releasing a successful product, Cisco is always looking ahead, anticipating the next big challenge in network security. Whether it's integrating artificial intelligence, automating threat responses, or developing solutions for new technologies like 5G, Cisco is always pushing the boundaries of what's possible. This commitment to innovation has made Cisco a true leader in the cybersecurity space, ensuring that their products not only meet the demands of today but are ready for the challenges of tomorrow. In a world where cyber threats evolve at breakneck speed, Cisco is always ahead of the curve, ensuring your network stays protected no matter what the future holds.

The Cisco Effect: Why Companies Trust Cisco for Network Security.

It's easy to see why Cisco is the go-to choice for so many organizations when it comes to network security. The company has earned its trust over decades by consistently delivering reliable, high-performance security solutions that meet the needs of businesses of all sizes. Whether you're a small business just getting started or a global enterprise with a complex network, Cisco has the tools and expertise to protect your data. Their products are scalable, customizable, and supported by one of the best customer service teams in the industry. Cisco's legacy of excellence, combined with its constant innovation, makes it the clear choice for those who take their network security seriously. In a world where the stakes are higher than ever, Cisco's products offer the protection and peace of mind every organization needs.

In Conclusion: Cisco's Heroic Journey in Network Security.

So, what's the takeaway here? Cisco is more than just a company—it's a superhero in the world of network security. It's the reliable sidekick you didn't know you needed, always there in the background, defending your digital empire with the quiet confidence of a true pro. From its foundational networking expertise to its cutting-edge security solutions, Cisco has earned its place as one of the top players in the field. Whether it's through its IDS/IPS systems, next-gen firewalls, or intelligent cloud security, Cisco's products work together in harmony to provide comprehensive protection. With Cisco at your side, you can rest assured that your network will remain secure, no matter what the future throws your way. So, here's to Cisco—the unsung superhero of network security, always ready to save the day when you need it most.

Chapter 3: Legacy Hardware – The Old-School Legends of Network Defense

1. **Ah, legacy hardware – the vintage car of network security.**
   There's something special about legacy hardware, isn't there? Sure, it's not as sleek or fast as the latest model, but it has character. It's like owning a classic muscle car that still runs perfectly (when you remember to turn the key just right). Back in the day, these legacy systems were the heavy hitters of network defense, holding their ground with the kind of durability and reliability that made them household names. While modern systems might have the cool factor and all the bells and whistles, legacy hardware had the grit and determination that made it a staple of network security. Think of it like your favorite grizzled detective—grumpy, a bit outdated, but always getting the job done. These devices may not win any beauty contests, but they were the unsung heroes that laid the foundation for all the sophisticated security technologies we rely on today.

2. **The Cisco PIX Firewall: The OG of Perimeter Defense.**
   Let's start with the Cisco PIX Firewall, the pioneer of perimeter defense. Back when it was first introduced in 1994, it was like the security guard who could spot a bad guy from a mile away. PIX wasn't fancy—it didn't have the bells and whistles of modern firewalls—but it worked like a charm, standing guard and keeping the riffraff out. It was simple, reliable, and didn't overcomplicate things. Back in the day, if you wanted a secure network, you needed a PIX firewall. While newer systems may have replaced it in many networks, the PIX firewall is like the foundation of a skyscraper—you don't see it anymore, but everything that's built on top owes it a huge debt. And, just like your dad's old car, it's probably still running in some server rooms, keeping the peace.

3. **Cisco ASA 5500 Series: A Bit More Modern, but Still a Classic.**
   Fast forward a decade, and the Cisco ASA 5500 Series comes onto the scene, bringing a little more modern flair to the mix. Introduced in 2005, the ASA 5500 series was like that reliable friend who finally upgraded from their flip phone to a smartphone—still dependable but with a little more functionality. It added intrusion prevention features, VPN capabilities, and more robust security features than its predecessor, the PIX. Cisco was starting to realize that people wanted a Swiss army knife for their security needs. The ASA 5500 was versatile, giving businesses not just firewalls but a multi-layered defense that was ahead of its time. It was like the "cool" parent at the PTA meeting—still rocking the classics but with a few modern upgrades to keep things interesting.

4. **The ASA 5500 Series: The Swiss Army Knife of Network Security.**
   One of the things that made the ASA 5500 Series stand out was its ability to combine multiple features into a single appliance. You could get a firewall, VPN, and intrusion prevention in one box, and that's where the ASA really shined. It was like owning a kitchen gadget that could chop, blend, and cook your dinner all in one. With built-in threat intelligence, firewalling, VPNs, and even a little bit of deep packet inspection, the ASA 5500 was a versatile, all-in-one device that delivered everything you needed to secure your network. While modern systems have far surpassed its capabilities, it still

holds a special place in the hearts of those who experienced the joy of configuring it in its heyday. If you ever found yourself setting up an ASA, you probably felt like you were in the cybersecurity equivalent of assembling IKEA furniture—there was a learning curve, but once you got it right, you felt pretty darn proud.

5. **The Legend of the Catalyst 6500: The Network Switch That Could.**
Before we dive deeper into firewalls and intrusion detection, let's take a detour and talk about the Cisco Catalyst 6500 Series. Introduced in 1999, the Catalyst 6500 was a switch that could handle everything—firewalls, intrusion prevention, and even wireless access. It was like the multi-tool of networking—except it didn't require any batteries, and it never got lost in your junk drawer. This switch became the backbone of many networks, offering scalability and flexibility that was unheard of at the time. It's also probably the most "unsung" hero of Cisco's lineup, often overshadowed by flashier firewalls and appliances. But without the Catalyst 6500, many of the more sophisticated security systems would never have been able to thrive. It's like the silent partner who keeps the business running, even though no one's paying attention.

6. **PIX and ASA: They Might Be Gone, But They're Never Forgotten.**
If you're reading this and wondering if PIX and ASA are still relevant, you're not alone. Many organizations still rely on these legacy systems, even as the industry moves to next-gen firewalls and cloud-based solutions. And why not? These systems might be "vintage," but they're still tough as nails. They've been through thick and thin, weathered countless cyberattacks, and proven their reliability time and time again. While Cisco no longer actively supports the PIX, and the ASA is transitioning into the Firepower line, many companies continue to use them in smaller environments or as a backup solution. They're like the classic rock bands of the network security world—maybe not making the charts anymore, but still beloved by a loyal fanbase.

7. **The End of an Era: Cisco's Transition to Next-Gen Firewalls.**
As much as we love our legacy hardware, the world has moved on, and so has Cisco. With the rise of more sophisticated threats, Cisco needed something more than what the PIX and ASA could offer. Enter the next-gen firewalls, like the Cisco Firepower Series. These devices bring everything you loved about legacy systems—like reliable firewalls and VPN support—but with the addition of deep packet inspection, advanced malware protection, and threat intelligence integration. It's like moving from a trusty old sedan to a brand-new sports car: you still get where you need to go, but now you're doing it with more horsepower. While we'll always have a soft spot for legacy hardware, the future of network security lies in these next-gen devices that can handle today's more complex and evolving threats.

8. **The PIX Firewall: An "Old Reliable" That Did More Than Its Fair Share.**
Let's circle back to the PIX firewall for a moment because, honestly, it deserves a standing ovation. It was simple, straightforward, and could be counted on to block traffic and prevent unauthorized access. Back in the 90s, when hacking was still in its infancy and cybercrime hadn't yet evolved into a global business, the PIX was the unsung guardian of corporate networks. It didn't need advanced algorithms or flashy UI—just

solid, hard-working protection that kept bad guys out. The PIX didn't need to show off. It did its job and did it well. While you might not see it as often today, its legacy is embedded in the very fabric of modern network security solutions.

9. **The ASA 5500 Series: When the "50 Shades of Security" Trend Started.**
Remember the time when every security device felt like it came with a thousand settings, each more complex than the last? Welcome to the world of the ASA 5500 Series. With its impressive range of configurations, the ASA Series really kicked off the trend of "50 shades of security," offering not just firewall functionality but the ability to customize almost every aspect of your network defense. Want to deploy a VPN? Check. Need an intrusion prevention system? Check. Want to inspect application traffic? Oh yeah, check that too. The ASA 5500 gave security professionals the power to fine-tune their defenses, but it also came with a steep learning curve. It was like an old-school manual transmission car—once you learned how to drive it, you felt like you could conquer the world, but until then, it took a bit of work.

10. **The Cisco Catalyst 6500: A Legacy That Still Lives On.**
As we mentioned earlier, the Cisco Catalyst 6500 Series was the rock star of network switches for many years. Even though newer models like the Catalyst 9000 series have emerged, the 6500 is still in use today in many organizations. This isn't just because people are nostalgic for the old days—though let's be honest, we all love a little retro flair —it's because the Catalyst 6500 was built to last. It was designed to handle massive amounts of traffic, integrate multiple security functions, and scale as needed. Even as technology advances, the Catalyst 6500 remains a reliable workhorse for many networks. Its legacy is a testament to the idea that if you build something well, it can withstand the test of time.

11. **The PIX Firewall: More Than Just a Box of Rules.**
You might think that the PIX firewall was just a box of rules and policies that stopped traffic at the edge of the network. But what really made it special was the way it enforced those rules with brutal efficiency. The PIX didn't get bogged down with complicated algorithms or fancy UIs; it just did what it was supposed to do—block unauthorized access and prevent attacks. It didn't need a flashy logo or a catchy slogan to impress—it was the security equivalent of a no-nonsense bodyguard who wasn't interested in small talk. If you knew what you were doing, the PIX was your trusted ally. And while other security devices were still figuring out what they wanted to be when they grew up, the PIX was already out there getting the job done.

12. **The ASA 5500: The Firewall That Wore Many Hats.**
The ASA 5500 Series wasn't just a firewall—it was a Swiss army knife of network security. It provided everything from firewall protection to VPNs to intrusion prevention and everything in between. With the ASA 5500, you could throw pretty much any security challenge at it, and it would respond with the appropriate tool. It was like a one-stop-shop for network security, which is why it became so popular in enterprise environments. It also brought a little more flexibility into the picture, with the ability to

deploy different security modules based on your organization's needs. In many ways, the ASA 5500 was the security multitasker before "multitasking" was even cool.

13. **PIX and ASA: The Giants That Built the Modern Firewall.**
When we look back at the history of firewalls, we can trace a direct line from the early days of the PIX to the more advanced Cisco Firepower series of today. The PIX and ASA firewalls may not have the sophistication of modern solutions, but they were groundbreaking in their time. They were the pioneers that established the best practices for intrusion detection, prevention, and network security in general. If it weren't for the lessons learned from the PIX and ASA, we wouldn't have the robust, AI-powered firewalls we have today. Sometimes the road to innovation is built on the shoulders of these legacy giants.

14. **Legacy Firewalls: A Part of Network Security's DNA.**
As much as we love shiny new gadgets, there's something to be said for legacy firewalls. These devices were the foundation of much of what we rely on today. They laid the groundwork for intrusion detection, prevention, and the overall architecture of secure networks. In fact, some of the basic concepts we use in modern firewalls were born from the necessity of these older systems. Even though we've moved on to newer, faster technologies, the lessons and principles established by the likes of PIX and ASA are still the bedrock of network security practices today.

15. **The Digital Graveyard: Where Legacy Devices Go to Rest (Not Forgotten).**
So, what happens to legacy hardware when it's no longer in use? Well, just because a device is "outdated" doesn't mean it gets tossed in the trash. In many organizations, legacy systems live on in secondary roles, often used for smaller networks or as backup devices. Sometimes, they end up in the "digital graveyard" of technology, gathering dust in server rooms, only to be resurrected when an emergency arises. But let's be real—just because they're not being actively used doesn't mean they're forgotten. These legacy systems still have value and are respected for what they contributed to the evolution of network security. You can retire them, but you can't erase their impact.

16. **The ASA 5500 Series: The Vintage Suit That Still Fits.**
In the world of fashion, certain styles never go out of fashion—like the classic black suit. The ASA 5500 is that suit of network security—still fitting into modern networks and providing valuable protection. Even though there are newer options available, the ASA 5500's versatility and reliability make it an attractive choice for some networks. It's the dependable, all-around device that's been trusted for years to handle everything from VPNs to malware protection. And while you might not want to wear a tuxedo to a casual gathering, the ASA 5500 is still the go-to security solution for many organizations that need something solid, dependable, and flexible.

17. **The Final Word on Legacy Devices: They Were Never "Just" Old Technology.**
Legacy devices like the PIX and ASA were never just "old technology." They were, and still are, critical pieces of the puzzle that helped build the digital security landscape we know today. They may have been replaced by newer systems, but they set the stage for innovations in firewall technology, intrusion detection, and network protection. While

newer tools may offer flashier features or more sophisticated threat detection, the core principles that made PIX and ASA successful are still relevant. These legacy devices were the pioneers of their time—no longer flashy, but never irrelevant. They paved the way for the future, and for that, we owe them a debt of gratitude.

The ASA 5500: Still the Old Soldier in Many Networks.
While newer systems like Cisco Firepower have taken the spotlight, the ASA 5500 continues to serve as the backbone of many businesses' network security. For small to medium enterprises or businesses that haven't upgraded yet, the ASA 5500 still does the job and does it well. It's like that old soldier who's seen countless battles and may not be as fast as the younger recruits, but you can count on it to step up when needed. The ASA 5500 doesn't offer the latest AI-driven threat analysis, but it can still block attacks, manage traffic, and provide VPN services with the best of them. And let's be honest: the familiarity and reliability of a tried-and-true device often outweigh the temptation to rush into the latest model. Some systems just have that old-school charm that makes them hard to part with, and the ASA 5500 is one of them.

The PIX Firewall: The Security Equivalent of Your First Car.
Remember your first car? It was probably a little rough around the edges, maybe even a little embarrassing, but it took you where you needed to go. That's the PIX firewall in a nutshell—it wasn't flashy, it wasn't the newest tech on the block, but it got the job done. Back in the day, when it hit the market, it was one of the best in the business. Its simplicity was its strength, and for many companies, the PIX was the first "security" device that allowed them to implement a more robust defense than just relying on basic router filters. Like your first car, the PIX might have a few dings and scratches, but it's still the security vehicle that started it all for many organizations. It's a testament to how far the industry has come, but also to how foundational those "early days" were in shaping modern cybersecurity.

The Transition from PIX to ASA: The Pivotal Moment in Firewall Evolution.
The shift from PIX to ASA wasn't just a simple product upgrade—it was a seismic change in the world of network security. The ASA series brought advanced features that PIX could never have dreamed of, like integrated VPNs, better application visibility, and intrusion prevention. This transition marked a pivotal moment in the evolution of firewalls and security appliances. But just like any transition, it wasn't without growing pains. Administrators had to learn how to migrate from the familiar (and simple) PIX interface to the more powerful, but complex, ASA configuration. It's a bit like going from playing a board game with your grandma to a complicated video game with real-time strategy. Sure, you're going to lose a few rounds at first, but once you get the hang of it, you realize you're playing in a whole new league.

The PIX and ASA Firewalls: The Foundation of Modern Threat Detection.
Before we had intelligent firewalls that could automatically detect and mitigate zero-day attacks, there were systems like the PIX and ASA that laid the foundation for modern threat detection. These legacy devices taught us the importance of combining multiple layers of defense, such as Stateful Packet Inspection (SPI) and Network Address Translation (NAT), to prevent malicious traffic from entering the network. They might not have had the fancy machine learning or AI capabilities that modern solutions offer, but they were smart enough to deal with most attacks of their time. It's like the basic principles of self-defense—they may not be as flashy as some of the

advanced martial arts moves, but they work and they're effective. As cybersecurity has grown in complexity, the lessons learned from these devices remain crucial for building more advanced, adaptive systems today.

Recycling Legacy Hardware: The Trend That Never Dies.
You've probably heard of "upcycling" in the world of fashion, but legacy network security hardware has its own version: recycling. Even as companies move to more advanced solutions, many keep legacy hardware around for backup purposes. The PIX and ASA firewalls may have been replaced by more modern appliances in your main network, but they still have plenty of life left in them when used in secondary roles. Perhaps they're monitoring smaller segments of the network, providing redundant protection, or just serving as a backup if your new system goes down. Recycling legacy hardware isn't just a way to save costs—it's also a way to preserve valuable lessons learned from years of security challenges. After all, a solid foundation never goes to waste.

Security by Simplicity: Why the PIX and ASA Were So Effective.
In today's world, everything seems to be about complexity. Firewalls now come with deep packet inspection, advanced behavioral analytics, and machine learning-powered threat mitigation. But there's a charm in simplicity—something that the PIX and ASA understood well. These firewalls didn't try to be everything to everyone; they focused on doing a few things really well: inspecting traffic, blocking unauthorized access, and keeping the network secure. And let's face it—sometimes the simpler solutions are the most effective. They didn't need to be "cutting-edge" to be valuable; they just needed to be solid, reliable, and focused on the basics of network security. Sometimes, that's all you really need.

The Enduring Value of Legacy Systems in Today's Complex Networks.
In today's complex networks, legacy systems like the PIX and ASA still have an enduring value. They might not have the capabilities to keep up with the latest threat vectors or provide real-time insights into deep packet inspection, but they continue to be useful for many networks that don't require the most advanced features. Legacy systems can still do a great job protecting smaller or less critical segments of your network. They're like the trusty old tool you keep in your toolbox —even if it's not the newest model, it's reliable and gets the job done. The reality is that not every network needs cutting-edge technology. For some, legacy firewalls are still perfectly capable of providing the necessary protection, and they're a cost-effective option that many organizations continue to rely on.

Final Thoughts: Legacy Devices Are the Grandparents of Modern Security.
In the grand scheme of network security, legacy devices like the PIX and ASA firewalls might be seen as the "grandparents" of modern security tools. They might not be the fastest, the flashiest, or the most advanced, but they're the ones who set the stage for everything that followed. Without these pioneering devices, the world of modern firewalls and intrusion detection systems might look very different. It's important to appreciate the legacy of these old-school security tools—not just for what they were but for what they allowed the industry to become. So, the next time you encounter one of these old devices, take a moment to acknowledge the contribution they've made to the evolution of network security. After all, even the most modern solutions owe a debt to the tried-and-true foundations laid by legacy hardware.

Chapter 4: Cisco Firepower 1000 Series – Meet the Rookie with a Punch

1. **Enter the Cisco Firepower 1000 Series: The New Kid in Town.**
   When it comes to network security, you usually hear about the tried-and-true, battle-tested appliances that have been around for decades. But every now and then, a fresh face arrives on the scene, ready to shake things up. Enter the Cisco Firepower 1000 Series, the rookie with a punch. Launched to bridge the gap between enterprise-grade and small-to-medium business (SMB) security, the Firepower 1000 Series brought a much-needed burst of power and flexibility to the market. Imagine a young prodigy who walks into the room and suddenly shows all the veterans how it's done. Cisco's Firepower 1000 Series is that kid—ready to mix it up and prove it's no lightweight when it comes to defending your network.

2. **Why SMBs Need the Firepower 1000 Series.**
   Let's be real—SMBs don't always have the resources to deploy the heavy-duty, enterprise-grade security appliances that large organizations use. But that doesn't mean they should settle for less when it comes to defending their networks. The Firepower 1000 Series fills that gap perfectly, delivering robust security without the sticker shock. Small businesses no longer need to compromise on performance or capabilities just because they're not a Fortune 500 company. The Firepower 1000 Series brings the best of both worlds: the power of next-gen firewall (NGFW) technology, along with intrusion prevention, all packed into a compact, cost-effective package. It's like giving your network the security equivalent of a lightweight champion—quick, agile, and powerful enough to go toe-to-toe with the bad guys.

3. **The Power Behind the Punch: Hardware That Packs a Punch.**
   Under the hood, the Cisco Firepower 1000 Series isn't just a pretty face—it's got the muscle to back up its reputation. Powered by an impressive CPU and backed by dedicated security processors, it handles threat detection, traffic inspection, and policy enforcement like a pro. You won't find any "sluggish" performance here. It's optimized for high throughput, which means it can keep up with the demands of growing businesses without breaking a sweat. With up to 5 Gbps of firewall throughput and 1.5 Gbps of intrusion prevention system (IPS) throughput, the Firepower 1000 Series is no slouch when it comes to handling high traffic loads. It's like the digital equivalent of a professional athlete—sleek, fast, and ready to compete with the best.

4. **Firepower 1000: It's Not Just a Firewall, It's a Next-Gen Powerhouse.**
   We all know firewalls are a critical part of network security, but the Firepower 1000 Series doesn't just stop there. It's a next-gen firewall (NGFW), which means it goes beyond traditional packet filtering. It includes advanced threat detection features such as deep packet inspection (DPI), URL filtering, application visibility, and more. This isn't your granddad's firewall—it's a sophisticated multi-functional appliance that can handle modern threats. With an integrated IPS, real-time traffic monitoring, and the ability to detect advanced malware, it provides a comprehensive security suite that goes far beyond what old-school firewalls can offer. Think of it like a Swiss Army knife for your network —it's got everything you need to keep your data safe and sound.

5. **Intrusion Prevention: The Bouncer at the Digital Door.**
The Cisco Firepower 1000 Series doesn't just open the door for traffic; it also has a bouncer standing at the entrance. That bouncer? The intrusion prevention system (IPS), which actively blocks malicious traffic in real-time. The IPS feature goes beyond simply detecting threats—it takes immediate action, preventing them from entering your network. It's like having a bouncer who checks IDs, kicks out troublemakers, and ensures no one with bad intentions gets through the door. This proactive defense is key to stopping attacks before they cause damage, and it works in tandem with the firewall's filtering to provide a dual layer of protection. If someone's trying to sneak in, the Firepower 1000 Series isn't having it.

6. **Threat Intelligence: Keeping You Ahead of the Game.**
The Firepower 1000 Series isn't just reactive; it's also proactive, thanks to its built-in threat intelligence capabilities. Powered by Cisco Talos, one of the largest commercial threat intelligence teams in the world, it has access to a constant stream of up-to-date information on the latest threats. This allows the system to quickly adapt to emerging cyber threats, keeping your network safe from the latest attack techniques. Think of it like having a crystal ball that tells you exactly when and where the next cyberattack is coming from—and knowing how to prevent it before it hits. Thanks to this threat intelligence integration, you can rest assured that your Firepower 1000 Series appliance is always in the know and ready to protect your network from the latest dangers.

7. **Easy Deployment: Get Set Up and Start Protecting.**
One of the best things about the Firepower 1000 Series is its ease of deployment. You don't need to be a networking wizard to get it up and running. With Cisco's intuitive interface and streamlined setup process, you can have the appliance configured and protecting your network in no time. It's designed with small businesses in mind, so the learning curve is minimal, even for those without a dedicated security team. The Firepower 1000 Series provides a smooth user experience, allowing businesses to focus on what matters most—growing their operations—without worrying about their security infrastructure. It's like having a security system that's so easy to use, even your non-tech-savvy colleague could set it up.

8. **Visibility and Reporting: Because You Can't Protect What You Can't See.**
What good is a security system if you can't see what it's protecting? The Firepower 1000 Series comes with a powerful reporting and monitoring system that provides real-time visibility into network traffic, threat activity, and security performance. The system includes detailed logs and visual analytics that make it easy to understand what's happening on your network. With these reports, you can identify patterns, uncover potential threats, and quickly respond to incidents. It's like having a security camera system with a live feed that lets you monitor everything happening in and around your digital property. And when the inevitable "security incident" happens, you'll be able to quickly trace the source, identify the impact, and take action.

9. **Scalability: Grown-Up Security for a Growing Business.**
As businesses grow, so do their security needs. The Firepower 1000 Series is built with

scalability in mind, allowing businesses to expand their security coverage as their networks grow. Need to add more devices, increase throughput, or expand your protection to new locations? No problem. The Firepower 1000 Series can scale with your organization, offering easy upgrades and flexibility as your needs change. It's like buying a suit that fits perfectly today but can be tailored tomorrow when you need a little more room. With the Firepower 1000 Series, you don't need to worry about outgrowing your security system—it's designed to grow with you.

10. **Advanced Malware Protection: Catching the Sneaky Stuff.**
Hackers love to use sneaky malware to worm its way into your network undetected. With Cisco's Firepower 1000 Series, you get advanced malware protection (AMP) that detects, blocks, and removes malicious software. AMP provides an additional layer of protection against viruses, worms, ransomware, and other types of malicious payloads. It works by continuously analyzing files, assessing their behavior, and comparing them against known threats. Think of it like having an undercover agent embedded in your network, looking for suspicious activity and taking down malware before it has a chance to spread. It's a constant game of cat and mouse, and with AMP, you always win.

11. **The Simplicity of Cisco's Firepower Management Center.**
Managing network security can feel like a juggling act, but the Firepower 1000 Series makes it easier with Cisco's Firepower Management Center (FMC). FMC provides a centralized platform to monitor and manage multiple Firepower devices across your network, so you can see everything from one place. Whether you have one Firepower appliance or multiple, FMC helps you keep track of everything that's going on, making it easier to enforce policies and respond to threats. It's like having a control center where you can pull all the levers and push all the buttons without getting lost in a sea of menus. With FMC, managing your Firepower appliances becomes streamlined and efficient, making security management a breeze.

12. **Firepower 1000 vs. the Competition: Why Cisco Wins.**
When you look at the competition, the Cisco Firepower 1000 Series stands out for its combination of performance, features, and price. Compared to other SMB-targeted firewalls, the Firepower 1000 offers a superior mix of next-gen security features, like intrusion prevention, malware protection, and advanced traffic analysis, while maintaining high throughput. It's like going to a high-end buffet that offers all-you-can-eat variety without charging you a premium. The competition may offer basic firewall features or lower-level protection, but Cisco has combined all the essentials into a single, affordable solution. It's not just about the hardware; it's about giving you the most bang for your buck, ensuring your network is protected without breaking the bank.

13. **Firewall as a Service: The Future of Security.**
While the Firepower 1000 Series is a physical device, Cisco is also paving the way for "Firewall as a Service" (FWaaS), which can integrate with cloud-based infrastructures. This is a growing trend in network security, and it's perfect for businesses looking to scale quickly while keeping their security infrastructure agile and manageable. By integrating Firepower 1000 Series with cloud-based solutions, businesses can offload

traffic inspection, threat detection, and policy enforcement to the cloud, reducing on-site hardware dependency. It's like having a flexible, elastic firewall that can expand or contract with your needs, all while maintaining a consistent level of protection. Whether you want to keep things local or push your security to the cloud, Cisco gives you the flexibility to do both.

14. **The Real-World Benefits of Firepower 1000 in Action.**
What's it really like to deploy a Firepower 1000 Series in the wild? Ask any small-to-medium-sized business that has implemented the device, and they'll tell you the same thing: it's a game-changer. The Firepower 1000 Series provides an excellent balance of simplicity and power, allowing businesses to deploy sophisticated security features without an IT team of 50. It's great for organizations that are scaling quickly or businesses that don't have the luxury of a massive security budget. Firepower 1000 doesn't just protect your network; it empowers your team by providing visibility, control, and real-time alerts when something goes wrong. It's like giving your network a personal bodyguard who's always watching, ready to step in at a moment's notice.

15. **Cost-Effective Security Without Compromise.**
Many businesses fear that robust security solutions will come with a hefty price tag. But Cisco's Firepower 1000 Series proves that doesn't have to be the case. This appliance is priced competitively for small businesses, delivering next-gen security features without the eye-watering costs associated with larger enterprise systems. For the price of a decent laptop, you can get an appliance that offers intrusion prevention, malware detection, application visibility, and real-time monitoring. It's a cost-effective option for businesses that want top-tier security without breaking the bank. For many SMBs, it's a no-brainer—affordable security that doesn't sacrifice quality.

16. **No More One-Size-Fits-All: Customizable Security with Firepower.**
One of the things that makes the Firepower 1000 Series stand out is its customizability. Unlike other security solutions that provide a one-size-fits-all approach, Firepower allows you to tailor the system to your network's unique needs. Whether you're securing a small office with a few employees or a rapidly expanding business with multiple branches, the Firepower 1000 Series can be customized to meet your security needs. From defining traffic rules to setting application-level policies, Cisco gives you the flexibility to protect what matters most. This kind of customization ensures that your security system adapts to your business, not the other way around.

17. **Firepower 1000's Role in Compliance: Ensuring Peace of Mind.**
Security isn't just about protecting against cyber threats; it's also about ensuring compliance with industry regulations. Whether you're in healthcare, finance, or retail, regulations like PCI-DSS, HIPAA, or GDPR require businesses to implement specific security measures to protect customer data. Cisco's Firepower 1000 Series plays an important role in helping businesses meet these compliance standards. With built-in security controls like traffic encryption, malware protection, and real-time monitoring, the Firepower 1000 ensures that businesses stay on the right side of the law. It's like

having a compliance officer and a network security expert rolled into one—ready to make sure your business stays secure and compliant without a second thought.

18. **Looking to the Future: Firepower 1000 as a Launchpad for Your Security Strategy.**
As businesses continue to grow, so do their security needs. The Firepower 1000 Series isn't just a "one-and-done" solution—it's designed to grow with your network. By investing in this next-gen firewall now, businesses lay the foundation for a scalable, future-proof security strategy. As your organization adds more devices, applications, and remote users, the Firepower 1000 Series can evolve to meet those challenges. Cisco has engineered this device with the understanding that today's security tools need to scale seamlessly into tomorrow's digital landscape. If you're thinking ahead, the Firepower 1000 is an ideal starting point for building a more robust security infrastructure as your business expands.

19. **The Verdict: Cisco Firepower 1000 Series Delivers More Than You Expect.**
When you first look at the Firepower 1000 Series, it may seem like a relatively simple appliance designed for small businesses. But what you quickly realize is that it punches well above its weight. With its advanced threat detection, real-time monitoring, and flexible deployment options, the Firepower 1000 Series offers capabilities that rival much larger, more expensive appliances. It's like the lightweight boxer who may not look intimidating but has the knockout punch to take down a champion. If you're a small-to-medium business looking for robust security without breaking the bank, the Firepower 1000 is the ultimate underdog story—a device that defies expectations and delivers security like a pro.

20. **Why Cisco Firepower 1000 Is the Ideal Choice for SMBs.**
The Firepower 1000 Series is tailor-made for SMBs—offering advanced features typically reserved for large enterprises, but at a price that's accessible for smaller organizations. Cisco understands that SMBs don't always have the resources to deploy the largest, most expensive security solutions, so they designed the Firepower 1000 to offer essential, next-gen security features in a compact package. Whether you're concerned about intrusion detection, advanced malware, or encrypted traffic, this device has you covered. For SMBs, the Firepower 1000 Series provides the ideal mix of functionality, scalability, and cost-effectiveness—making it a wise investment for growing businesses looking to secure their future.

21. **Easy Integration with Cisco's Broader Security Ecosystem.**
If you're already using Cisco's security tools, integrating the Firepower 1000 into your existing infrastructure is a no-brainer. With Cisco's streamlined ecosystem, the Firepower 1000 Series integrates seamlessly with other Cisco products, making it easier to expand your network security without complicated setups. This compatibility extends to Cisco's cloud-based security tools, threat intelligence feeds, and the Firepower Management Center (FMC). It's like adding another layer to your already rock-solid defense—without the hassle. Thanks to Cisco's focus on interoperability, you don't have to worry about your security tools not playing well together. Instead, you can rest easy knowing your systems will work in perfect harmony.

22. **Firepower 1000 for Remote Work: The Security Solution You Need.**
With remote work becoming the norm for many organizations, securing remote users has never been more important. The Firepower 1000 Series offers a range of features that ensure secure connectivity for remote workers, including VPN support, threat detection, and encrypted traffic inspection. It's like having a virtual bodyguard for each employee who's working from home, ensuring that their data and devices are protected wherever they are. For businesses that are embracing remote work, the Firepower 1000 Series is the security solution you need to keep your network safe in a decentralized world.

23. **The Bottom Line: Affordable, Powerful Security for the Modern Network.**
The Firepower 1000 Series isn't just a great option for SMBs—it's an excellent choice for any business looking for affordable, high-performance network security. With its combination of next-gen firewall capabilities, advanced threat detection, and easy deployment, the Firepower 1000 Series provides everything you need to keep your network safe. It's the perfect balance of cost, functionality, and scalability, making it a powerful tool for organizations looking to future-proof their security. When it comes to getting the most value for your money, the Firepower 1000 Series delivers a knockout punch, offering robust protection without the hefty price tag.

24. **Firepower 1000: The Real MVP for Small Businesses.**
Let's be honest—security for small businesses often gets overlooked. They tend to get caught in the "cheap and easy" trap, opting for subpar solutions that don't provide adequate protection. But the Firepower 1000 Series changes the game. It offers SMBs the kind of protection that was once reserved for large enterprises, without the massive investment. Whether you're just starting out or scaling your operations, the Firepower 1000 is the MVP of network security for small businesses. It gives you the tools and protection you need to stay safe and secure, while still fitting into your budget.

25. **In Conclusion: Meet the Firepower 1000 – Your Network's New Best Friend.**
In the world of cybersecurity, finding the right balance of power, performance, and affordability isn't always easy. But with the Cisco Firepower 1000 Series, you get all of that—and more. Whether you're an SMB just getting started or a growing business looking to scale, this appliance provides the kind of security that punches well above its weight. With next-gen firewall features, intrusion prevention, threat intelligence integration, and more, the Firepower 1000 Series offers everything you need to keep your network safe from evolving threats. It's the rookie with a punch, ready to take on anything the bad guys throw its way—and come out victorious.

Chapter 5: Cisco Firepower 2100 Series – Leveling Up Security Like a Pro

1. **Meet the Cisco Firepower 2100 Series: The Next Step in Network Security.**
When you think of network security, you're probably picturing the most sophisticated, cutting-edge technologies out there. Now, let's level up your imagination a bit—enter the Cisco Firepower 2100 Series. This device isn't just an upgrade; it's an evolution in the world of intrusion prevention and next-gen firewall solutions. Imagine the Firepower 1000 Series as the rookie with a punch, and the Firepower 2100 Series as the seasoned pro stepping onto the scene with more power, flexibility, and advanced features. If the

1000 Series was a promising college athlete, the 2100 is now a seasoned pro, ready to take on the toughest competition. With faster processing, better scalability, and more advanced threat protection, the Firepower 2100 Series brings network security into the big leagues. It's like stepping up from the minors to the major leagues—without missing a beat.

2. **Performance Boost: Bigger, Faster, Stronger.**
    You know what they say: "Go big or go home." Cisco took that advice to heart with the Firepower 2100 Series, packing a massive performance upgrade compared to its predecessor. With up to 10 Gbps of firewall throughput and 3 Gbps of IPS throughput, this device can handle the highest demands of modern business networks. If the Firepower 1000 was like a car you could comfortably drive around the city, the Firepower 2100 Series is a high-performance sports car, engineered for speed and power. Whether you're monitoring traffic for threats, applying complex policies, or processing encrypted traffic, the Firepower 2100 doesn't break a sweat. It's like a personal trainer for your network—getting faster, stronger, and more efficient every time you push it to the limit. So, if you're dealing with growing traffic loads or more complex security needs, the Firepower 2100 is the upgrade that gives you the muscle you need.

3. **Why Scalability Matters – Because Your Network Isn't Staying the Same Size Forever.**
    As your network grows, so does your need for robust security that can scale with you. The Firepower 2100 Series is built to handle that growth. It's not just a firewall; it's a security platform designed to grow with your business. Whether you're expanding your team, opening new locations, or implementing more cloud-based services, the Firepower 2100 Series can scale to meet those evolving needs. With its modular architecture, it's like getting a security solution that can grow with you, rather than forcing you to keep buying new devices every time your network gets bigger. The Firepower 2100's flexibility ensures you're prepared for both the present and the future, making it an investment that can evolve as your company's demands change. Because let's face it—if your network isn't growing, you're probably doing something wrong.

4. **Advanced Threat Protection: The Ultimate Defense Against Advanced Attacks.**
    When it comes to network security, the bad guys are always getting more sophisticated. Enter the Firepower 2100 Series with its advanced threat protection capabilities that take security to a whole new level. With features like advanced malware protection (AMP), deep packet inspection (DPI), and real-time intrusion prevention, the Firepower 2100 is like having a cybersecurity expert at your side, 24/7. It doesn't just look for known threats; it actively hunts for suspicious patterns, zero-day vulnerabilities, and emerging attack techniques. The Firepower 2100 isn't just reacting to attacks; it's anticipating them, stopping threats before they even get a chance to spread. It's like having a security guard who not only stops criminals at the door but also reads their minds to figure out what they're going to do next.

5. **The Power of Cisco's Threat Intelligence: Staying Ahead of the Curve.**
    The Firepower 2100 Series isn't just smart—it's *connected* to the world's largest threat

intelligence network, Cisco Talos. Talos is a team of world-class researchers and cybersecurity experts constantly gathering data, analyzing threats, and identifying new attack methods. This gives the Firepower 2100 Series access to real-time intelligence that helps it predict and block threats before they even hit your network. It's like having a security expert who doesn't just react to threats—they see them coming from miles away. Cisco Talos integrates seamlessly with the Firepower 2100, ensuring that your defenses are always up to date and your network stays one step ahead of the bad guys. So, while the attackers are busy plotting their next move, Cisco's got the playbook—and the Firepower 2100 is running interference.

6. **Firepower 2100 Series and the Cloud: Perfecting the Hybrid Security Approach.**
In today's digital landscape, businesses operate in hybrid environments, with a mix of on-premises and cloud-based infrastructure. The Firepower 2100 Series is built for this reality, providing comprehensive security across both environments. Whether your applications are running in the cloud or your data is stored on-prem, the Firepower 2100 provides seamless protection for both. It integrates with Cisco's cloud security solutions, allowing you to extend your security policies to the cloud without adding complexity. Think of it like building a security perimeter that spans both your office and the digital cloud—you're protected everywhere, and you don't need to worry about gaps in your coverage. The Firepower 2100 Series makes hybrid security easy, allowing you to manage everything from one central platform.

7. **Simple, Centralized Management with Firepower Management Center (FMC).**
You could have the most powerful security appliance in the world, but if it's a pain to manage, what's the point? Luckily, the Firepower 2100 Series comes with Cisco's Firepower Management Center (FMC), which makes managing multiple devices a breeze. FMC provides a unified interface where you can monitor, configure, and respond to security incidents across your entire network. Whether you have one Firepower 2100 or an entire fleet of them, FMC simplifies the process, allowing you to manage everything from one dashboard. It's like having a control center where you can adjust your security settings on the fly, view real-time threat activity, and quickly respond to incidents without switching between different tools. With FMC, managing your network's security becomes a well-organized, efficient process, leaving you more time to focus on what matters most.

8. **The Power of Automation: Because Who Has Time for Manual Work?**
Let's face it—network security is a 24/7 job. But you don't have to do all the heavy lifting yourself, thanks to the Firepower 2100's powerful automation features. Cisco has built advanced automation into the Firepower 2100, allowing the system to respond to threats in real-time without requiring you to constantly intervene. Whether it's applying security updates, blocking malicious traffic, or adjusting policies based on new threat data, the Firepower 2100 handles it all automatically. This not only reduces the workload for your security team but also speeds up response times, ensuring that your network stays protected without delay. It's like having an assistant who never sleeps, doesn't need lunch breaks, and never makes mistakes—talk about a time-saver.

9. **Multi-Layer Security: Because One Layer Isn't Enough.**
In the world of cybersecurity, defense-in-depth is the name of the game. The Firepower 2100 Series is built with multi-layered security, meaning that it doesn't just protect at one point; it secures your network from multiple angles. With features like advanced threat protection, VPN support, deep packet inspection, and IPS, the Firepower 2100 offers a robust and comprehensive defense. The system isn't just trying to stop attacks from getting in; it's analyzing traffic at every layer, looking for patterns and behaviors that suggest something isn't quite right. By applying multiple layers of security, the Firepower 2100 Series ensures that your network is protected even if one layer is bypassed. It's like having multiple security guards, each with a different skill set, ensuring no bad guy gets through.

10. **Flexibility in Deployment: Your Network, Your Rules.**
One of the great things about the Firepower 2100 Series is its flexibility in deployment. Whether you need a traditional perimeter firewall, a VPN concentrator, or an inline IPS, the Firepower 2100 can be deployed in various ways to meet your organization's specific needs. It offers flexible form factors for rack-mounted or standalone deployments, allowing you to choose the best setup for your environment. And because it integrates with other Cisco security tools, you can build a custom solution that fits your network like a glove. It's like choosing the perfect tool for the job—you get to decide how you want to deploy and manage your security, based on your business's unique requirements.

11. **Firepower 2100 and IoT: Securing the Connected World.**
The Internet of Things (IoT) is rapidly expanding, and with it, the number of devices connecting to your network is growing exponentially. The Firepower 2100 Series is built to handle this influx of IoT traffic, providing the same level of protection for your connected devices as it does for traditional endpoints. From sensors to smart devices to wearables, the Firepower 2100 can protect all the IoT devices that are part of your network ecosystem. It's like having a security system that's ready for the future, protecting devices that didn't even exist a few years ago. As the IoT landscape continues to evolve, Cisco's Firepower 2100 ensures that your network can grow and adapt to new technologies without sacrificing security.

12. **Visibility is Key: Real-Time Insights into Your Network.**
One of the standout features of the Firepower 2100 Series is its ability to give you detailed, real-time insights into your network activity. From monitoring traffic flow to identifying potential threats, the Firepower 2100 provides actionable intelligence that helps you stay on top of network health and security. Think of it like a dashboard in a luxury car—while you're driving, it gives you all the critical information you need at a glance. The visibility provided by the Firepower 2100 allows you to identify potential threats before they become problems, helping you maintain a secure and optimized network. It's like having a crystal ball that shows you exactly what's happening in your digital world.

13. **Advanced Malware Protection (AMP): Keeping the Bad Stuff Out.**
The Firepower 2100 Series is packed with advanced malware protection (AMP) that

helps detect and block the most dangerous types of malicious software. AMP goes beyond traditional signature-based detection by analyzing file behavior and patterns, even looking for new malware variants that haven't yet been identified. It's like having a team of cybersecurity experts who are constantly searching for new and evolving threats and neutralizing them before they can do damage. Whether you're dealing with ransomware, trojans, or worms, AMP ensures that your network stays protected from malware that could slip past other defenses. With AMP, you're not just reacting to threats; you're actively preventing them.

14. **The Evolution of the ASA: The Firepower 2100 Series is the New Standard.**
If you've been in the network security game for a while, you're probably familiar with Cisco's ASA series. The ASA was a great firewall, but the Firepower 2100 Series takes things to a whole new level. It builds on the strengths of the ASA, adding modern capabilities like better performance, advanced malware protection, and cloud integration. Think of it like upgrading from a classic car to a high-tech hybrid: the Firepower 2100 keeps the same reliability of the ASA but adds cutting-edge features to ensure you're ready for the future. The transition to the Firepower 2100 Series isn't just about getting a faster, more powerful device; it's about staying ahead of evolving threats and leveraging Cisco's next-gen security technologies.

15. **Cost vs. Value: Getting More Bang for Your Buck.**
When it comes to investing in network security, many businesses wonder whether they're getting their money's worth. The Firepower 2100 Series strikes the perfect balance between cost and value. It offers enterprise-grade security features at a price point that's accessible for mid-sized businesses, giving you the protection you need without breaking the bank. When you consider the features—advanced malware protection, real-time threat detection, and cloud integration—the value proposition becomes crystal clear. With the Firepower 2100, you're getting more than just a firewall; you're getting a comprehensive security solution that scales with your business and helps you stay secure in an ever-changing threat landscape.

16. **Next-Gen Security: Future-Proofing Your Network.**
The Firepower 2100 Series isn't just built for today—it's built for the future. With features like cloud integration, advanced malware protection, and integration with Cisco's broader security ecosystem, this device is ready for whatever comes next. Whether it's an evolving threat landscape, the rise of 5G, or the growing demand for cloud-based services, the Firepower 2100 is prepared to adapt. Cisco has designed this series with the understanding that the cybersecurity landscape is always changing, and businesses need to be able to respond quickly and effectively. When you invest in the Firepower 2100, you're not just buying a product for today; you're future-proofing your security infrastructure for years to come.

17. **Deployment Made Easy: Because Security Shouldn't Be Complicated.**
Setting up a next-gen firewall doesn't have to be a headache. The Firepower 2100 Series is designed for quick and easy deployment, with Cisco's intuitive setup process and comprehensive user guides. You don't need to be a network wizard to get started. With

automated installation processes and clear instructions, you can get your device up and running without spending hours on configuration. Whether you're a small business or a growing enterprise, Cisco's focus on simplicity ensures that security doesn't need to be complicated. It's like buying a high-performance sports car with a user-friendly interface —power, speed, and simplicity, all in one package.

18. **Bringing the Power of Cisco Security into Your Hands.**
Cisco has built a legacy of providing robust, enterprise-grade security tools, and the Firepower 2100 Series brings that power into the hands of businesses of all sizes. With its high throughput, advanced threat protection, and easy-to-use interface, the Firepower 2100 makes enterprise-level security accessible to mid-sized businesses. It's like taking a top-tier security system from a Fortune 500 company and making it available for the small guy. No matter your company's size, the Firepower 2100 ensures you get the same level of protection as the biggest names in the business.

19. **Firepower 2100 and Compliance: Keeping You on the Right Side of the Law.**
Compliance is a big deal in many industries. Whether you're in healthcare, finance, or retail, staying compliant with regulations like GDPR, HIPAA, or PCI-DSS is essential. The Firepower 2100 Series helps you meet these regulatory requirements by offering a robust set of security features, such as data encryption, intrusion prevention, and malware detection, all of which help you protect sensitive data and ensure that your network remains compliant. With the Firepower 2100 on your side, you can focus on growing your business, knowing that your security infrastructure has got your back when it comes to compliance.

20. **The Final Word: Cisco Firepower 2100 Series – The Pro's Choice for Next-Gen Security.**
In the world of network security, the Cisco Firepower 2100 Series is a game-changer. With its advanced capabilities, impressive performance, and ease of use, it's the perfect solution for businesses that need enterprise-level protection without the complexity. Whether you're securing your on-premises network, protecting remote workers, or expanding into the cloud, the Firepower 2100 Series delivers the security and performance you need to stay ahead of the competition. It's time to level up your security —because the Firepower 2100 Series is ready to take your defenses to the next level.

Smarter Security with Real-Time Analytics.

One of the greatest strengths of the Cisco Firepower 2100 Series is its ability to provide real-time analytics, which gives you the insight you need to act before problems arise. It's like having a surveillance system that not only lets you see everything happening in your network but also analyzes it instantly, flagging potential risks before they become full-blown threats. With this level of visibility, you can identify abnormal traffic patterns, spot suspicious behavior, and even predict future threats based on historical data. In the fast-paced world of cybersecurity, this real-time feedback is invaluable—it allows your team to respond faster, make better decisions, and stay a step ahead of cybercriminals. So, while others might still be reacting to threats, your Firepower 2100 is already stopping them in their tracks.

Security That Grows with Your Business.
As your company evolves, so do your security needs. The Firepower 2100 Series offers seamless scalability, allowing it to grow as your business does. Whether you're adding new users, expanding your network, or moving more services to the cloud, the Firepower 2100 can scale to meet your changing demands. This scalability ensures that you won't have to go through the headache of replacing your security infrastructure as your business expands. It's like getting a security solution that grows alongside your business, giving you the flexibility and adaptability needed to stay secure no matter how big you get. With the Firepower 2100, you're not just buying a firewall; you're investing in a long-term security partner that will evolve as your needs change.

The Power of Deep Packet Inspection: Because Surface-Level Security Doesn't Cut It.
In the world of cybersecurity, shallow inspections are a recipe for disaster. That's why the Firepower 2100 Series is built with deep packet inspection (DPI) to look inside every packet that enters or leaves your network. DPI goes beyond the basics, examining the content of packets to ensure that no malicious data gets through. It's like having a security guard who doesn't just check the ID but also opens the suitcase to make sure no one's sneaking in contraband. This advanced inspection capability allows the Firepower 2100 to detect threats that other, less sophisticated systems might miss—whether they're hidden in encrypted traffic or disguised as legitimate data. With DPI, you can rest assured that your network is being meticulously monitored for any signs of trouble.

The Firepower 2100: A Complete Security Suite for Your Network.
Security isn't just about keeping the bad guys out; it's also about understanding and controlling what's going on inside your network. The Firepower 2100 Series acts as a complete security suite that combines next-gen firewall protection, intrusion prevention, malware detection, and application visibility into one device. It's like having a team of highly trained security professionals working around the clock, watching every corner of your network and ensuring nothing slips through the cracks. With the Firepower 2100, you're not just getting a firewall, you're getting an entire security ecosystem that's designed to detect, block, and analyze threats from every angle. It's comprehensive protection that gives you the confidence to know your network is safe from every possible attack vector.

Why You Should Trust the Firepower 2100 Series: Cisco's Reputation Precedes It.
In the world of cybersecurity, trust is everything. Cisco has built a reputation over decades as one of the most reliable names in networking and security. The Firepower 2100 Series is no exception—it builds on Cisco's legacy of excellence and combines it with the latest innovations in threat protection. With Cisco's years of expertise behind it, the Firepower 2100 delivers a level of security that's hard to match. Cisco's customer service and technical support are second to none, and the Firepower 2100 Series benefits from continuous updates and improvements through Cisco's global threat intelligence network, Talos. When you invest in a Cisco product, you're not just buying a device; you're getting a trusted partner that's committed to keeping your network safe from evolving threats.

Advanced Malware Protection (AMP): Not Just for Malware, But for the Future.
If there's one thing we've learned in cybersecurity, it's that malware evolves quickly. But with

the Firepower 2100 Series, you're not just protecting your network from today's malware—you're future-proofing your security against tomorrow's threats. Cisco's Advanced Malware Protection (AMP) continuously monitors your network, proactively detecting and blocking malware before it can do any damage. AMP goes beyond traditional detection methods by analyzing the behavior of files and network traffic, ensuring that even unknown threats are identified and neutralized. This proactive approach ensures that your network is ready for any new type of malware that emerges, giving you an edge over the cybercriminals who are always looking for new ways to slip past defenses.

No More Silos: How the Firepower 2100 Integrates with Your Other Cisco Security Tools.
One of the most powerful features of the Firepower 2100 Series is its ability to integrate seamlessly with Cisco's broader security ecosystem. Cisco's security tools aren't isolated; they communicate with each other, sharing data and threat intelligence to enhance your overall security posture. This integration allows you to manage all aspects of your network security from a centralized platform, streamlining your processes and improving overall efficiency. Whether you're managing endpoint protection, firewalls, or threat intelligence feeds, everything works together in harmony. It's like having a symphony where all the instruments play in perfect harmony—without the noise or confusion that often comes with siloed security solutions.

The Real Benefits of Cloud Integration with Firepower 2100.
In today's world, cloud computing is no longer a luxury; it's a necessity. With businesses increasingly moving critical operations to the cloud, ensuring that your cloud-based data and applications are secure is more important than ever. The Firepower 2100 Series integrates seamlessly with Cisco's cloud-based security solutions, providing visibility and protection across both on-premises and cloud environments. Whether your data lives in a private cloud or a hybrid environment, the Firepower 2100 ensures that your entire network is protected, no matter where it resides. This cloud integration gives you the flexibility to scale your security as your cloud infrastructure grows, making it easier to maintain comprehensive protection across all your assets.

Tailored Security: Customizing the Firepower 2100 for Your Network.
Every business is different, and so is every network. That's why the Firepower 2100 Series offers customizable security policies that can be tailored to fit the specific needs of your network. Whether you need to block certain types of traffic, prioritize bandwidth for specific applications, or create custom intrusion prevention rules, the Firepower 2100 lets you configure it all. This level of customization ensures that your security settings match your unique network requirements, providing protection without unnecessary complexity. It's like having a tailor-made suit that fits perfectly—providing you with a level of comfort and protection that off-the-rack solutions can't match.

Security Visibility for the Entire Network: No Blind Spots.
Visibility is key when it comes to network security. The Firepower 2100 Series gives you detailed, granular visibility into all the traffic flowing through your network. This means you can track everything—from routine data transfers to suspicious activity—without any blind spots. With features like application visibility and control (AVC), you can gain deeper insights into how applications are using your network, identify potential vulnerabilities, and enforce policies that

ensure secure communication. Having this level of visibility allows you to take proactive action, such as blocking harmful traffic before it can spread, or optimizing bandwidth for critical applications. It's like having a security camera system with a bird's-eye view of everything happening on your network.

The Firepower 2100 and the Growing Threat of Ransomware.
Ransomware is one of the biggest threats to modern organizations, and its prevalence is only increasing. Fortunately, the Firepower 2100 Series offers a range of defenses to help combat this malicious threat. With advanced malware protection, intrusion prevention, and continuous monitoring, the Firepower 2100 can detect and block ransomware before it has a chance to encrypt your files and demand a ransom. It's like having a security system that stops ransomware in its tracks, preventing a potentially devastating attack before it starts. The Firepower 2100 Series actively analyzes all traffic and files, ensuring that no ransomware can infiltrate your network undetected.

The Future-Proofing Advantage: The Firepower 2100 as a Long-Term Investment.
In the fast-evolving world of network security, it's crucial to make long-term investments that will remain relevant as your organization grows and the threat landscape changes. The Firepower 2100 Series is designed with future-proofing in mind. It's built to handle not only the challenges of today but also the emerging threats of tomorrow. With its modular design, advanced features, and constant updates via Cisco's Talos threat intelligence network, the Firepower 2100 ensures that your investment will continue to protect you for years to come. Whether you're moving to the cloud, adding IoT devices, or expanding your business globally, the Firepower 2100 will grow with you, providing robust security no matter what comes next.

Cisco's Reputation for Excellence: Why Trust Matters.
When it comes to cybersecurity, trust is non-negotiable. That's why Cisco's longstanding reputation in the networking and security industries is such an important factor when choosing the Firepower 2100 Series. Cisco has spent decades building a track record of reliable, high-performance security solutions, and the Firepower 2100 is no exception. By choosing Cisco, you're selecting a company that's committed to providing top-tier security, continuous innovation, and world-class customer support. With Cisco, you know you're getting a trusted, proven partner that will help keep your network safe from evolving threats. It's like hiring a security firm with decades of experience—they've got the skills and the expertise to protect you.

The Firepower 2100 Series: The Complete Security Solution.
When you're looking for a security appliance, you want a solution that provides everything you need in one package. The Firepower 2100 Series delivers just that. It combines next-gen firewall protection, intrusion prevention, advanced malware protection, and seamless cloud integration into a single device. With its modular design and powerful capabilities, it's the complete security solution for businesses that want to stay protected, no matter where they're located or how complex their network is. Whether you're defending against traditional attacks or modern threats like ransomware, the Firepower 2100 offers the protection your network deserves. It's like having a full-service security team, all wrapped up in one device.

Final Thoughts: The Firepower 2100—Your Next-Level Security Solution.
In the world of network security, there's no such thing as being too prepared. The Cisco

Firepower 2100 Series takes your network defense to the next level, providing powerful protection that's scalable, flexible, and designed for modern threats. From advanced threat protection to real-time visibility and cloud integration, the Firepower 2100 has everything you need to secure your network both now and in the future. It's an investment in your organization's security that will pay dividends for years to come. So, if you're ready to level up your security, the Firepower 2100 Series is the solution that will take you to the next level. It's the kind of security that not only keeps up with today's challenges but anticipates tomorrow's threats—ensuring your network is always protected, no matter what comes next.

Chapter 6: Cisco Firepower 4100 Series – Big, Bad, and Ready to Defend

1. **Meet the Cisco Firepower 4100 Series: The Heavyweight Champion of Network Security.**
   When you're dealing with critical enterprise environments, there's no room for second-rate security appliances. Enter the Cisco Firepower 4100 Series: the heavyweight champion of network defense, designed to handle the toughest, most complex security challenges. It's big, it's bad, and it's built to take on the most demanding security workloads. This isn't a device you casually slap into a small business; the Firepower 4100 Series is for those who need serious muscle to defend against sophisticated threats. Think of it as the security equivalent of a seasoned bodyguard—always on alert, never dropping the ball, and more than capable of handling whatever comes its way. It's engineered to protect enterprise networks at scale, delivering unmatched performance, visibility, and control. If your network was a fortress, the Firepower 4100 would be the moat, the drawbridge, and the heavily armed guards rolled into one.

2. **The Performance Beast: Speed, Power, and Efficiency.**
   One of the most impressive aspects of the Firepower 4100 Series is its raw performance. With up to 26 Gbps of firewall throughput and 9 Gbps of IPS throughput, this device is built for speed and high-performance security. Whether you're handling massive amounts of traffic, running complex inspection rules, or managing high-bandwidth applications, the Firepower 4100 keeps things running smooth. It's like driving a luxury sports car that's built for both speed and reliability—when you push it, it doesn't break a sweat. In an era where network demands are increasing at an unprecedented rate, the Firepower 4100 Series gives you the peace of mind knowing your security system can handle it all without compromising performance. From traffic inspection to threat detection, it's fast, efficient, and doesn't let anything slip through the cracks.

3. **Scalability: Security That Grows With You.**
   The Firepower 4100 Series isn't just powerful—it's also highly scalable, designed to meet the evolving needs of large enterprises. As your organization grows, so do your security demands, and Cisco's Firepower 4100 Series is built to scale seamlessly. Need to expand your protection to more locations, additional users, or increased traffic load? No problem—the Firepower 4100 can handle it all. It's like a security system that grows with you, without needing to be replaced every time your business takes the next step. With flexible configurations and modular architecture, you can add more performance or

functionality as needed, ensuring that your security keeps pace with your network. You won't outgrow this appliance anytime soon.

4. **The Flexibility to Meet Any Network Challenge.**
    One of the things that sets the Firepower 4100 Series apart from the competition is its flexibility. Whether you need it as a traditional perimeter firewall, an inline intrusion prevention system (IPS), or a VPN concentrator, this appliance can be easily configured to meet your specific needs. It's like a Swiss Army knife for network security, allowing you to customize it to protect your network in exactly the way you need. The Firepower 4100 Series is built to handle a variety of security challenges and can be deployed in different architectures, from branch offices to complex data centers. Need to deploy it in a high-availability pair or integrate it into a larger security fabric? It's ready for that too. Its adaptability ensures it fits into any part of your security infrastructure, no matter how complex.

5. **Advanced Threat Protection: Ready for the Big Leagues.**
    When it comes to defending against advanced persistent threats (APTs), zero-day attacks, and other sophisticated malware, the Firepower 4100 Series is ready to go toe-to-toe with the best. It comes equipped with Cisco's next-gen firewall capabilities, advanced malware protection (AMP), and intrusion prevention system (IPS), which means it's not just monitoring for known threats—it's actively hunting them down. It's like having a top-tier cybersecurity team on the front lines, constantly scanning for new vulnerabilities and actively stopping threats in their tracks. Whether you're dealing with known threats or new, emerging attack vectors, the Firepower 4100 Series is equipped to protect your network from every angle. With the power of Cisco's Talos threat intelligence and continuous updates, this system stays ahead of the curve, anticipating attacks before they happen.

6. **Comprehensive Visibility: Seeing the Whole Picture.**
    You can't protect your network if you don't understand what's happening inside it. That's why the Firepower 4100 Series is designed to provide comprehensive visibility into your network traffic. With advanced monitoring tools and detailed reporting, you get a complete view of your network's activity, enabling you to identify threats, track suspicious behavior, and optimize performance. Cisco's Firepower Management Center (FMC) centralizes all of this information, providing you with a single pane of glass to monitor and manage security across your entire network. It's like having a security camera system that not only lets you watch but also provides detailed insights into what's happening across every corner of your network. Real-time visibility gives you the intelligence you need to make informed decisions and respond to threats before they become a problem.

7. **Integration with Cisco's Security Ecosystem: A Unified Defense.**
    One of the key advantages of the Firepower 4100 Series is how seamlessly it integrates into Cisco's broader security ecosystem. Whether it's integrating with Cisco's Umbrella for cloud security, Talos for threat intelligence, or your existing endpoint protection systems, the Firepower 4100 Series acts as the backbone of a unified, end-to-end security

strategy. It's like having a superhero team where every member plays a key role in protecting your network—each tool and appliance working together to provide maximum protection. This integration allows you to create a security fabric that spans your entire organization, providing a holistic approach to threat defense. With Cisco's ecosystem, you can rest easy knowing your security tools aren't working in isolation; they're all communicating and sharing data to stop threats faster and more effectively.

8. **Cost-Effective Security for Large Enterprises.**
   For large enterprises, investing in top-tier security doesn't always come with an enterprise-level price tag. The Firepower 4100 Series offers an excellent balance of performance, security features, and cost-efficiency. You're getting enterprise-grade security without the sticker shock that often comes with larger appliances. While other solutions might require multiple devices or expensive add-ons to achieve the same level of protection, the Firepower 4100 Series provides everything you need in one scalable appliance. It's like buying a luxury car that offers all the bells and whistles, but without the hefty price tag. If you want top-of-the-line security without draining your IT budget, the Firepower 4100 is the solution that checks all the boxes.

9. **Handling Encrypted Traffic: Because HTTPS Isn't Enough.**
   Encrypted traffic is a growing concern in modern network security. While it's great for protecting data in transit, it's also a prime avenue for attackers to slip malicious payloads past traditional firewalls. The Firepower 4100 Series doesn't just let encrypted traffic bypass its defenses. With its ability to decrypt, inspect, and re-encrypt HTTPS traffic, it ensures that even encrypted data is thoroughly checked for threats. Think of it like having a security guard who not only checks for weapons at the door but also opens up all the sealed packages to make sure nothing dangerous is hiding inside. The Firepower 4100's ability to handle encrypted traffic ensures that attackers can't use encryption as a loophole to sneak past your defenses.

10. **Firepower 4100 and VPNs: Securing Remote Connections with Ease.**
    In today's world, remote work is no longer just a perk; it's the norm. As businesses embrace remote workforces, securing those connections becomes a top priority. The Firepower 4100 Series makes it easy to secure remote connections with advanced VPN capabilities. Whether you need to implement site-to-site VPNs for branch offices or secure remote access for employees, the Firepower 4100 Series has got you covered. It's like giving your remote workers a secure tunnel into your network—allowing them to work efficiently without compromising security. And with advanced encryption, you can rest assured that their traffic remains safe from prying eyes, whether they're working from a coffee shop or a home office.

11. **The Power of Automation: Because Nobody Likes Busywork.**
    One of the key benefits of the Firepower 4100 Series is its automation capabilities. In the fast-paced world of cybersecurity, responding to threats in real-time is critical—but you can't afford to burn out your team with manual tasks. The Firepower 4100 Series automates many routine security processes, including threat detection, policy enforcement, and updates. It's like having a security assistant who does all the grunt work

while you focus on the big picture. Automated threat detection and responses help ensure that your network remains secure without requiring constant manual intervention. This not only improves your response time but also frees up your security team to focus on more strategic tasks. With the Firepower 4100 Series, automation allows you to stay ahead of the game while keeping your team productive.

12. **Seamless High Availability: Because Downtime Isn't an Option.**
In an enterprise environment, downtime is a luxury that few can afford. The Firepower 4100 Series is designed with high availability in mind, ensuring that your security infrastructure stays up and running even in the event of a failure. With features like automatic failover and redundant power supplies, the Firepower 4100 Series ensures that your network stays protected 24/7. It's like having a backup security team on standby, ready to jump in at a moment's notice if something goes wrong. By implementing high availability, the Firepower 4100 minimizes the risk of downtime, ensuring that your network stays secure no matter what. And since you're in control, you can easily monitor the health of your devices and proactively address issues before they become critical.

13. **Ready for the Future: The Firepower 4100 and Emerging Technologies.**
Cybersecurity is a constantly evolving field, and businesses need security solutions that can keep pace with emerging technologies. The Firepower 4100 Series is designed with the future in mind, offering the flexibility to adapt as new technologies—like 5G, SD-WAN, and IoT—become more prevalent. Whether you're dealing with increased traffic from mobile devices or securing new services running on a 5G network, the Firepower 4100 is ready to handle it. This future-proofing capability ensures that you won't need to constantly replace your security appliances as your network evolves. It's like investing in a system that's not only secure today but is also equipped to defend against tomorrow's threats, no matter how advanced they may be.

14. **Security Without Compromise: The Firepower 4100's No-Nonsense Approach.**
With so many security appliances on the market, it's easy to feel overwhelmed by the choices. But the Firepower 4100 Series cuts through the noise, providing a no-compromise security solution for enterprises. It doesn't try to be everything to everyone; it just focuses on what matters most: high-performance, scalable, and reliable network protection. Whether you're securing a sprawling network or a critical data center, the Firepower 4100 offers everything you need without overcomplicating things. It's like getting the perfect tool for the job—effective, efficient, and ready to deliver results without all the fluff. For enterprises that want top-tier security without unnecessary features, the Firepower 4100 is the solution you've been waiting for.

15. **Firepower 4100: The Unseen Defender of Your Network.**
The best security solutions often work in the background, quietly protecting your network without you even realizing it. The Firepower 4100 Series is one of those solutions. While it's delivering top-notch protection, detecting threats, and managing traffic, it does so with minimal disruption to your network operations. It's like a security guard who's so good at their job that you don't even notice they're there. The Firepower 4100 Series

provides comprehensive protection without slowing down your business operations, ensuring that your network stays safe without compromising on performance.

16. **High-Level Customization: Tailoring Security to Your Needs.**
No two networks are the same, and that's why the Firepower 4100 Series offers extensive customization options. From configuring policies based on your unique business requirements to adjusting security protocols to fit your specific use case, the Firepower 4100 allows you to tailor the appliance to meet your needs. Whether you're prioritizing certain applications or blocking specific types of traffic, the Firepower 4100 lets you configure your security exactly how you need it. Customization ensures that you're not just applying a one-size-fits-all security approach—you're building a defense that's designed for your business and its unique challenges. With this level of control, you can create a security solution that truly fits your needs.

17. **Protecting Your Critical Assets: The Firepower 4100's Core Mission.**
For any enterprise, protecting critical assets is priority number one. Whether it's sensitive customer data, intellectual property, or financial records, you need a security solution that ensures those assets are kept safe from malicious actors. The Firepower 4100 Series provides advanced protection for all your critical assets by blocking known threats and identifying new ones before they can cause damage. It's designed to detect threats at every layer of your network and prevent unauthorized access to your valuable resources. With the Firepower 4100, you're putting a powerful defender in place that's constantly vigilant, protecting your network's most important assets with the highest level of security available.

18. **Firepower 4100 in Action: Real-World Results.**
It's one thing to talk about how powerful the Firepower 4100 Series is, but the real test comes when it's deployed in the real world. Customers who have implemented the Firepower 4100 Series in their environments report significant improvements in security posture, with fewer successful attacks, reduced false positives, and better network performance. Whether it's blocking advanced malware, detecting encrypted threats, or preventing unauthorized access, the Firepower 4100 delivers in spades. It's not just talk— it's real-world results that demonstrate the true power of this appliance. When you deploy the Firepower 4100, you're not just getting a security solution; you're investing in a reliable defense system that works.

19. **The Power of Cisco's Global Threat Intelligence: Always on the Offensive.**
Cybercriminals are constantly evolving, but Cisco's global threat intelligence network, Talos, is always one step ahead. Talos constantly analyzes data from around the world, identifying new threats and vulnerabilities in real time. This valuable intelligence is integrated directly into the Firepower 4100, ensuring that your security is always based on the most up-to-date threat data. When new attacks are discovered, Talos works tirelessly to update the Firepower 4100, ensuring that you're always protected against the latest threats. It's like having a worldwide network of security experts constantly working to keep your network safe, all integrated into your security system.

20. **Seamless Integration with SIEM Systems: Data-Driven Security Management.**
A great security solution is only as effective as the data it can collect and analyze. The Firepower 4100 Series integrates seamlessly with Security Information and Event Management (SIEM) systems, allowing for centralized monitoring, logging, and alerting across your entire network. By feeding real-time data from the Firepower 4100 into your SIEM system, you gain deeper insights into your security environment, enabling faster response times and more accurate threat analysis. This integration enhances your ability to spot patterns, correlate events, and proactively respond to incidents. It's like connecting the dots—when all your security systems are working together, you get a clearer picture of what's going on across your entire network.

21. **Ready for the Future: The Firepower 4100 Series Is Built for Tomorrow.**
The Firepower 4100 Series isn't just designed for today—it's built for the future. With support for emerging technologies, like cloud computing, SD-WAN, and 5G, the Firepower 4100 is ready to handle whatever comes next. As businesses continue to adopt new technologies, the Firepower 4100 ensures that your security infrastructure remains adaptable, scalable, and future-proof. Whether you're expanding to the cloud, integrating IoT devices, or preparing for the next-gen networks of tomorrow, the Firepower 4100 Series is ready to defend against evolving threats without missing a beat.

22. **Cost vs. Value: Why the Firepower 4100 Delivers Exceptional ROI.**
Investing in a high-performance security appliance can be a tough decision for many organizations, but when you consider the value the Firepower 4100 Series offers, it's easy to see why it's worth the investment. The combination of top-tier performance, scalability, and advanced threat protection ensures that your network is well-protected for years to come. Compared to other high-performance security solutions on the market, the Firepower 4100 delivers exceptional ROI, providing you with more bang for your buck. Whether it's reducing the risk of a breach, lowering your operational costs, or improving your network efficiency, the Firepower 4100 Series provides long-term value that makes it an investment that pays off.

23. **The Final Word: Firepower 4100 – Big, Bad, and Unstoppable.**
When it comes to securing large, high-performance networks, there's no room for compromise. The Cisco Firepower 4100 Series delivers exactly what enterprises need: power, flexibility, and cutting-edge security features that protect against today's and tomorrow's threats. With its robust performance, scalability, and seamless integration into your existing security infrastructure, the Firepower 4100 is ready to take your network defense to the next level. Big, bad, and always on guard, the Firepower 4100 Series is the heavyweight champion of network security. When you're ready to defend your organization with the best, the Firepower 4100 Series is here to answer the call.

24. **A Legacy of Protection: Cisco's Commitment to Security.**
Cisco has built a legacy of providing reliable, scalable, and powerful security solutions, and the Firepower 4100 Series is no exception. With decades of expertise behind every line of code and hardware configuration, Cisco's commitment to network security is evident in every aspect of the Firepower 4100. This series continues to build on Cisco's

reputation for providing industry-leading defense against the most advanced cyber threats. When you choose Cisco, you're choosing a company that has been at the forefront of network security for years, ensuring that your organization is always one step ahead of attackers.

25. **Your Next Step in Network Defense: The Firepower 4100 Series.**
So, what's the next step in securing your organization? It's simple: the Cisco Firepower 4100 Series. Designed for large enterprises that need the best protection, this device offers unmatched performance, scalability, and security. Whether you're dealing with high volumes of traffic, complex security needs, or the ever-evolving threat landscape, the Firepower 4100 has everything you need to defend your network with confidence. It's the big, bad security solution that's ready to take on anything—and it's here to stay.

Chapter 7: Cisco Firepower 9300 Series – The Big Guns of Network Defense

1. **Introducing the Cisco Firepower 9300 Series: The Big Guns of Network Defense.**
When it comes to defending large, mission-critical networks, sometimes you need more than just a solid defense—you need firepower. That's where the Cisco Firepower 9300 Series comes into play. This is no rookie player; it's the heavyweight champion of network defense, designed to tackle the biggest and baddest cyber threats head-on. If the Firepower 4100 Series is the reliable bodyguard, the 9300 Series is the bouncer who can handle a whole club full of unruly guests. With its unparalleled throughput, advanced threat protection, and scalability, the 9300 Series is designed to protect the most demanding environments. Whether you're a multinational corporation, a government agency, or a large data center, this appliance is built to deliver the performance and protection you need. Think of the Firepower 9300 as your network's personal bodyguard, heavy-duty armor, and traffic controller all rolled into one.

2. **Unmatched Performance: Because Fast Is Never Fast Enough.**
The Firepower 9300 Series doesn't just talk the talk—it walks the walk with some of the highest throughput and performance in the market. With up to 160 Gbps of firewall throughput and 25 Gbps of IPS throughput, this appliance is built to handle the most demanding network traffic without breaking a sweat. Whether your organization is running massive data centers, complex cloud environments, or high-speed enterprise networks, the 9300 Series ensures that your security appliances won't become a bottleneck. It's like the difference between a Ferrari and a minivan—you could get where you're going in a minivan, but a Ferrari will do it faster, with style, and without stalling. The Firepower 9300 ensures that as your network grows, your security system grows with it, maintaining speed and performance every step of the way.

3. **The Power of Modular Design: Flexibility Meets Power.**
One of the standout features of the Firepower 9300 Series is its modular design, allowing you to configure the system to meet your unique needs. Need more throughput? Add another module. Need additional network interfaces or storage? It's as easy as swapping out a component. This modularity ensures that the Firepower 9300 is more than just a "one-size-fits-all" solution; it's a customizable powerhouse that adapts to your network's evolving requirements. It's like having a high-end PC that you can upgrade as new

technology comes out—you don't need to throw away the whole system when you need more power; just add the right components. Whether you're scaling up for future growth or adapting to new traffic patterns, the Firepower 9300 Series provides the flexibility and performance you need to stay ahead of the game.

4. **Advanced Threat Protection: Not Just a Firewall, But a Fortress.**
   A firewall is great, but when you're dealing with advanced threats, you need something more than just basic protection. The Firepower 9300 Series is a next-gen firewall (NGFW) with built-in intrusion prevention (IPS), advanced malware protection (AMP), URL filtering, and more. It doesn't just monitor for threats; it actively hunts for them, stopping attacks before they even get a chance to damage your network. Whether it's blocking zero-day threats, detecting malware hidden in encrypted traffic, or preventing sophisticated phishing attacks, the Firepower 9300 Series ensures your network stays secure from every angle. It's like having a fortified wall around your digital kingdom, constantly reinforced with the latest threat intelligence. And, just in case you were wondering, Cisco's Talos threat intelligence network ensures that the Firepower 9300 is always prepared for the latest attack methods and techniques.

5. **The Heart of the Data Center: Built for High-Density Environments.**
   Large enterprises and data centers are often the targets of sophisticated cyberattacks, so they need security appliances that can handle massive amounts of traffic without flinching. The Firepower 9300 Series is built for high-density environments, providing high throughput and low latency to ensure that even the most complex data center operations are secure. It's engineered to handle the demands of large-scale deployments, providing consistent protection across your entire network while maintaining top-tier performance. Whether you're managing thousands of virtual machines, running high-traffic web applications, or supporting large databases, the Firepower 9300 is built to handle it all. It's like an all-terrain vehicle built to take on any terrain—smooth roads, rocky paths, or muddy marshes—and still keep moving forward without missing a beat.

6. **Visibility: The Power to See Everything.**
   When you're managing a large, complex network, visibility is crucial to maintaining security. The Firepower 9300 Series doesn't just provide visibility into the basics—it gives you full transparency into your network traffic, threats, and security posture. Cisco's Firepower Management Center (FMC) gives you a centralized platform to monitor all your Firepower devices, providing real-time insights into network activity, security events, and policy enforcement. Whether you're tracking traffic flows, identifying anomalies, or troubleshooting network issues, the Firepower 9300 ensures you have the tools you need to stay on top of your network's health and security. It's like having an air traffic control tower for your digital network, giving you the ability to direct and manage traffic with pinpoint precision.

7. **Integrated with Cisco's Security Ecosystem: A Unified Defense.**
   The Firepower 9300 Series doesn't just work in isolation—it's part of a larger security ecosystem that integrates with other Cisco products and services. From Cisco Umbrella for cloud security to Cisco Stealthwatch for network visibility, the Firepower 9300 Series

integrates seamlessly with Cisco's broader security suite. This integration enables you to create a unified defense across your entire organization, making it easier to monitor, respond to, and block threats across all points of your network. It's like building a fortress with multiple layers of security—each component working together to provide maximum protection. With this integrated approach, you don't have to worry about gaps in coverage or siloed security tools; everything works together in perfect harmony.

8. **Automated Threat Detection and Response: Because Speed is Everything.**
The Firepower 9300 Series takes threat detection and response to the next level by automating many of the routine tasks involved in network security. From automatically applying security updates to adjusting threat detection algorithms based on emerging data, the Firepower 9300 is always ready to respond to new and evolving threats. It's like having a highly skilled security guard who works tirelessly around the clock, without taking breaks or missing a beat. Automation reduces the time it takes to detect and respond to security incidents, allowing your team to focus on higher-level strategic tasks. The ability to react in real-time without human intervention is one of the most powerful features of the Firepower 9300—because, in cybersecurity, every second counts.

9. **Cloud Security: Extending Protection to the Cloud.**
The shift to the cloud has made network security more complex, but the Firepower 9300 Series is designed to handle this complexity. It integrates seamlessly with Cisco's cloud security solutions, allowing you to extend your protection beyond the data center to the cloud. Whether you're protecting cloud-based applications, securing hybrid environments, or managing access to cloud resources, the Firepower 9300 Series provides comprehensive protection across your entire infrastructure. It's like having a digital bouncer that ensures only authorized traffic enters the cloud, while blocking unwanted visitors before they cause any harm. With the rise of multi-cloud environments, the ability to extend security to the cloud is essential, and the Firepower 9300 Series delivers just that.

10. **High Availability: Keeping Your Network Secure 24/7.**
When it comes to network security, downtime is not an option. The Firepower 9300 Series is built with high availability in mind, providing redundancy and failover capabilities to ensure that your security infrastructure remains operational around the clock. Whether you're deploying it in an active/passive pair or as part of a larger, distributed security network, the Firepower 9300 ensures that if one device goes down, the other picks up the slack. It's like having a backup generator for your network security —if the power goes out, the protection never does. With this level of redundancy, you can be confident that your network is always secure, even in the event of a hardware failure or network disruption.

11. **Flexible Deployment: Ready for Any Environment.**
The Firepower 9300 Series offers flexible deployment options, ensuring it can meet the needs of your specific environment. Whether you need it as an inline IPS, a perimeter firewall, or a high-performance VPN concentrator, the Firepower 9300 can be configured to suit your needs. Its modular architecture also allows for easy upgrades and expansions,

so you can adjust your deployment as your business grows or your network changes. It's like having a security system that's built to fit the specific requirements of your business, rather than forcing you to adapt to a rigid solution. This level of flexibility ensures that the Firepower 9300 can seamlessly integrate into your existing infrastructure, no matter how complex.

12. **Advanced Malware Protection: Proactive Defense Against Ransomware and More.**
The Firepower 9300 Series provides advanced malware protection (AMP), which continuously monitors network traffic and endpoints to detect and block malicious files. This includes proactive defense against ransomware, viruses, trojans, and any other type of malware that might try to sneak past traditional defenses. AMP doesn't just look for known threats—it analyzes file behavior to identify new, unknown malware that hasn't yet been cataloged. It's like having an advanced AI system that's constantly learning, adapting, and blocking malicious activity before it can do any damage. Whether the malware is coming through email, infected websites, or encrypted traffic, AMP ensures that it never gets a chance to enter your network.

13. **Security Analytics and Reporting: Intelligence at Your Fingertips.**
With the Firepower 9300 Series, you get access to detailed security analytics and reporting that provide deep insights into your network's health and security posture. These reports give you the intelligence you need to identify vulnerabilities, track traffic patterns, and optimize network performance. Whether you're conducting a routine security audit, investigating an incident, or monitoring traffic in real-time, the Firepower 9300's reporting tools ensure that you have all the data you need at your fingertips. It's like having a security operations center (SOC) on your desktop, providing you with actionable intelligence and helping you make informed decisions about your network security. With Cisco's advanced analytics, you can see exactly what's going on in your network—and take immediate action when needed.

14. **Cost Efficiency for Large-Scale Deployments.**
You might think that with all its power, the Firepower 9300 Series would come with a hefty price tag. But Cisco has designed it with cost efficiency in mind, offering large-scale protection at a price point that makes sense for big enterprises. When you factor in its performance, scalability, and integration with Cisco's other security solutions, the Firepower 9300 delivers exceptional value. It's like buying a high-end sports car that has the performance you need without the extravagant price tag. For organizations that need to protect large, high-traffic networks, the Firepower 9300 Series provides the perfect balance of power, flexibility, and affordability.

15. **Security for the Entire Organization: End-to-End Protection.**
Whether you're protecting a small office or a global enterprise, the Firepower 9300 Series provides end-to-end protection for your entire organization. From securing branch offices to safeguarding data centers, the Firepower 9300 Series ensures that your network is defended from every angle. Its ability to integrate with other Cisco security products, like Umbrella and Stealthwatch, gives you a comprehensive security fabric that spans your entire organization. It's like having a security guard at every door, watching every entry

point, and constantly communicating to ensure your network is protected no matter where threats may arise.

16. **Designed for Future Threats: Evolving with the Threat Landscape.**
Cyber threats evolve at a rapid pace, but the Firepower 9300 Series is designed to evolve with them. Whether it's the rise of AI-driven attacks, the proliferation of IoT devices, or the adoption of new network technologies, the Firepower 9300 is built to handle emerging threats. Its modular design and continuous software updates ensure that your security infrastructure stays up-to-date with the latest threat intelligence and protection techniques. It's like a security system that's constantly adapting and evolving to stay one step ahead of the attackers. With the Firepower 9300 Series, you don't just protect against today's threats—you future-proof your network security for years to come.

17. **Real-Time Defense: Keeping Your Network Secure, 24/7.**
The Firepower 9300 Series offers real-time defense capabilities, allowing you to respond to attacks as soon as they happen. Whether you're blocking a DDoS attack, quarantining infected devices, or updating security policies, the Firepower 9300 is designed to act quickly and decisively. With real-time threat analysis and response, your network is always protected, even as new threats emerge. It's like having a team of security experts on-call at all hours of the day, ready to protect your network from any threat that might arise. This instant defense gives you the peace of mind that your network is always secure, 24/7.

18. **Effortless Integration with Your Existing Network Infrastructure.**
Implementing a new security appliance can sometimes feel like installing a square peg in a round hole. But with the Firepower 9300 Series, integration into your existing network infrastructure is seamless. Whether you're using traditional firewalls, routers, or advanced security solutions, the Firepower 9300 fits right in. It integrates easily with other network devices and works with your existing configurations to provide an added layer of protection. The Firepower 9300 Series doesn't disrupt your network—it enhances it, making your security stronger without adding unnecessary complexity. It's like finding the perfect puzzle piece that fits effortlessly into place, completing your network's security picture.

19. **Endless Customization: Tailoring the Firepower 9300 to Your Needs.**
No two businesses are the same, and the Firepower 9300 Series understands that. Whether you're securing an enterprise data center, protecting remote offices, or managing traffic for a large-scale cloud environment, the Firepower 9300 can be customized to fit your needs. From creating custom policies to prioritizing certain types of traffic, the 9300 Series allows you to define your security posture based on your unique requirements. It's like having a tailor who can adjust your suit until it fits perfectly—it's security that's designed just for you. Customization ensures that the Firepower 9300 doesn't just provide blanket protection; it offers a solution that's optimized for your network.

20. **Protection for Your Digital Transformation Journey.**
As businesses embark on their digital transformation journey, they face new challenges and risks, particularly around cybersecurity. The Firepower 9300 Series provides robust

protection as your organization migrates to the cloud, adopts new technologies, and scales its operations. Whether you're implementing SD-WAN, securing mobile devices, or enabling IoT, the Firepower 9300 offers comprehensive protection for every aspect of your digital transformation. It's like having a security expert by your side as you navigate the complexities of digital change, ensuring your network remains secure no matter where your journey takes you.

21. **Improving Efficiency: Reduced Complexity with Centralized Management.**
Managing security across large, complex networks can quickly become overwhelming. But with Cisco's Firepower Management Center (FMC), you can streamline and simplify the process. FMC offers centralized management for all your Firepower appliances, making it easier to monitor, configure, and respond to threats across your entire network. It's like having a control room where you can see everything happening across your network and take action instantly. FMC reduces the complexity of managing security at scale, allowing your team to focus on higher-level tasks instead of getting bogged down in day-to-day management.

22. **The Firepower 9300: A Long-Term Investment in Security.**
When it comes to network security, you don't want to just buy a solution for today—you want something that will continue to deliver value for years to come. The Firepower 9300 Series is designed with long-term performance and scalability in mind, making it an investment that pays dividends over time. With its modular architecture, continuous software updates, and seamless integration with Cisco's broader security ecosystem, the Firepower 9300 Series ensures that your security infrastructure remains adaptable and effective as your business grows and the threat landscape evolves. It's an investment in the future, ensuring your network stays secure no matter what changes are on the horizon.

23. **Conclusion: The Firepower 9300 – The Ultimate Defense for the Enterprise.**
When you need enterprise-grade security that can handle the toughest threats and the most demanding environments, the Cisco Firepower 9300 Series is the solution. With its high performance, advanced threat protection, scalability, and integration with Cisco's broader security ecosystem, the Firepower 9300 is built to defend against the most sophisticated cyberattacks. Whether you're protecting a data center, securing the cloud, or managing a large-scale network, the Firepower 9300 provides comprehensive, reliable protection for all your needs. It's the ultimate defense system for the enterprise—a powerful, adaptable solution that's ready to take on anything the digital world throws its way.

24. **The Power of Cisco's Threat Intelligence – Keeping Your Network Ahead of the Curve.**
Cisco's Talos threat intelligence network is one of the most comprehensive and advanced in the cybersecurity industry, providing your Firepower 9300 with the most up-to-date threat data. With this intelligence integrated into the Firepower 9300 Series, your network is always prepared for emerging threats. Whether it's a new variant of ransomware, a sophisticated phishing attack, or a zero-day vulnerability, Talos ensures that your

defenses are always prepared. It's like having a crystal ball that tells you exactly what threats to expect, so you can stop them before they even reach your network.

25. **Why the Firepower 9300 Is the Right Choice for Your Organization.**
The Firepower 9300 Series is the solution for large enterprises that need powerful, scalable, and highly effective network security. With its unmatched performance, advanced protection, and ability to scale as your business grows, the Firepower 9300 ensures your network stays secure no matter how complex or demanding your operations are. It's the ideal security appliance for organizations that need to protect critical infrastructure, manage high-traffic networks, and defend against sophisticated cyber threats. If you want the best in network security, look no further than the Firepower 9300 Series—because when it comes to defending your network, you deserve nothing less than the big guns.

Chapter 8: Cisco Firepower Management Center (FMC) – Central Command for Your Security Army

1. **Introduction to FMC: The General in Charge of Your Network Security.**
In a world where network security is a constant battle, you need more than just individual defenders; you need a command center that coordinates, monitors, and directs your security forces. Enter the Cisco Firepower Management Center (FMC), the general of your security army. FMC is the hub where all the action happens, bringing together your Firepower devices to provide unified security management. Think of it as the control room in a spy thriller—where all the data is funneled, analyzed, and then acted upon with precision and speed. Without FMC, your Firepower devices are like soldiers on the battlefield with no commanding officer. They might be effective on their own, but they won't be as coordinated or efficient. FMC ensures that every decision is backed by real-time data and intelligence, allowing your security teams to respond faster and more accurately. It's the central command that turns your security architecture into a well-oiled machine.

2. **The Power of Centralized Control: One Dashboard to Rule Them All.**
In large enterprises, managing multiple security devices across different networks can quickly become a nightmare. But with FMC, all your Firepower appliances are brought together in a single, centralized dashboard that provides a bird's-eye view of your network security. Gone are the days of jumping between different screens and interfaces —FMC puts everything you need at your fingertips. It's like having a remote control that lets you adjust the settings, track threats, and respond to incidents without having to leave your desk. The single-pane-of-glass view is the perfect metaphor for FMC—it's like a network security superhero, combining all the best tools into one convenient interface. Whether you're managing thousands of devices or just a handful, FMC ensures that your security posture remains in top shape, no matter how complex your environment.

3. **Real-Time Visibility: Knowing What's Happening, When It Happens.**
When your network is under attack, waiting for someone to notice the breach can be too late. That's why FMC provides real-time visibility into your entire security infrastructure. Whether it's inspecting traffic, identifying threats, or tracking network activity, FMC

provides immediate insights into what's happening on your network at any given moment. Imagine having a spy camera installed in every nook and cranny of your digital world, feeding live footage back to the control room. FMC provides this kind of clarity, allowing security teams to make faster, informed decisions. With its detailed reports, graphs, and visual analytics, FMC allows you to spot anomalies, monitor policy effectiveness, and track down threats in record time. It's the kind of visibility you need to stay ahead of cybercriminals, giving you the upper hand in the never-ending game of cat and mouse.

4. **Policy Management: Setting the Rules of Engagement.**
   Every good army has a set of rules that guide its actions—and your network is no different. FMC allows you to create, manage, and enforce security policies across all your Firepower devices. Want to block specific types of traffic? It's just a click away. Need to adjust VPN rules or configure intrusion prevention systems? FMC's policy management makes it easy to apply changes to the entire security infrastructure in one unified step. It's like having a playbook for your network's defense, ensuring that every device follows the same game plan. FMC also gives you the flexibility to fine-tune policies based on specific needs—whether that's creating rules for certain applications, enforcing tighter security for remote workers, or prioritizing traffic for critical services. With FMC, you're always in control of your security policies, ensuring that your network is defended exactly how you want it.

5. **Automated Threat Response: Less Waiting, More Action.**
   When a cyberattack occurs, seconds matter. The Firepower Management Center empowers your security infrastructure with automated threat detection and response capabilities. Imagine if your security system could automatically respond to threats without requiring you to lift a finger. That's exactly what FMC does—when a potential threat is detected, FMC can automatically block it, quarantine infected devices, or alert your security team in real-time. It's like having an elite tactical unit that doesn't wait for orders; it acts on its own to neutralize the threat and protect your network. Automated responses reduce the time between threat detection and mitigation, ensuring that your security measures are always proactive. With FMC, you don't have to wait for someone to notice the issue—you're already one step ahead.

6. **Advanced Reporting: The Data You Need, When You Need It.**
   As a security administrator, it's important to have access to detailed reports that show the effectiveness of your defenses, track incidents, and ensure compliance with regulations. FMC's advanced reporting capabilities provide just that—giving you granular insights into your network's security posture. Whether you're looking for high-level summaries or diving deep into specific security events, FMC delivers reports that are both comprehensive and customizable. Need to generate reports for an audit or compliance review? It's as easy as selecting the right template and clicking "generate." The best part? FMC offers real-time data reporting, ensuring that you can always see what's going on in your network—whether it's the last hour or the last 30 days. It's like having a detailed logbook that tracks everything happening in your network, so you can quickly pull up the data you need, when you need it.

7. **Threat Intelligence: The Tactical Advantage.**
   In the world of cybersecurity, knowledge is power—and with FMC, you gain access to Cisco Talos, one of the world's largest and most advanced threat intelligence teams. This integration ensures that your Firepower devices are always equipped with up-to-date, actionable intelligence on the latest threats. Talos continuously analyzes global threat data, and this intelligence is fed into FMC, keeping your defenses current and aware of emerging attack techniques. It's like having a group of expert spies working around the clock, providing you with intel on enemy movements and helping you adjust your defenses accordingly. With this kind of intelligence at your fingertips, you can proactively block new threats before they have a chance to infiltrate your network.

8. **Scaling Your Security with FMC: No Network Too Big.**
   As your organization grows, so does your network's complexity. The Firepower Management Center is designed to scale with your business, ensuring that you can manage even the largest, most complex network infrastructures. Whether you're expanding to new offices, managing multiple data centers, or handling increased traffic demands, FMC allows you to easily scale your security policies, monitoring, and device management across your entire organization. It's like having a single, powerful brain coordinating every aspect of your security, from local offices to global operations. With FMC, you don't need a separate tool for each part of your network—it consolidates everything into one unified management system, making it easier to monitor and defend against threats no matter where they originate.

9. **Centralized Device Management: One Hub to Rule Them All.**
   Managing multiple security devices can feel like a juggling act, especially when you're dealing with dozens or even hundreds of Firepower appliances. FMC simplifies this by allowing you to manage all your devices from a centralized platform. From configuring devices to monitoring their performance and security status, FMC lets you handle everything from one screen. Imagine trying to herd cats—now imagine that each cat is a critical part of your security system. FMC takes the chaos out of managing large networks, streamlining operations so your team can focus on what matters: keeping your network safe. Whether it's setting up new devices, applying updates, or responding to alerts, FMC makes it easy to keep everything running smoothly.

10. **Incident Investigation: Hunting Down the Culprits.**
    When a security breach happens, you need to investigate quickly to identify what happened, who was responsible, and how to prevent it from happening again. FMC provides powerful incident investigation tools that allow you to drill down into specific security events, analyzing the root cause of the issue. With detailed logs, historical data, and real-time traffic analysis, FMC enables you to track incidents from start to finish, providing a clear timeline of events. It's like playing detective, but with a high-tech magnifying glass that helps you zoom in on exactly what went wrong. By using FMC's investigation tools, you can quickly identify the threat's origin, its impact, and how it moved through your network, allowing you to mitigate the issue and strengthen your defenses moving forward.

11. **Flexible Deployment Options: Fit for Any Organization.**
    One of the reasons FMC is so popular is its flexibility. Whether you're running a small office network, a large enterprise, or a global infrastructure, FMC can be deployed to meet your needs. It can be run as a virtual appliance, integrated into the cloud, or installed on a dedicated physical server, depending on your organization's size and requirements. This flexibility ensures that FMC is accessible to businesses of all types and sizes, without requiring a complete overhaul of your existing infrastructure. It's like having a security system that can be customized to fit the exact shape and size of your organization, whether you're operating from a single location or multiple regions.

12. **Simplified Management with FMC's Intuitive User Interface.**
    Let's face it—no one wants to spend their days battling with a clunky, unintuitive security interface. FMC is designed to be as user-friendly as it is powerful, making it easy for security professionals of all skill levels to manage and configure security policies. With its clean, streamlined design, FMC ensures that you can get to what you need quickly and efficiently. The intuitive interface makes monitoring network traffic, investigating incidents, and managing security policies as easy as pointing and clicking. It's like upgrading from a manual transmission to an automatic—you can still drive the same fast car, but now you don't have to think about every gear change.

13. **Collaboration Made Easy: Security Teams, United.**
    Network security is rarely a solo job—it takes a team to defend against threats. FMC facilitates collaboration between your security teams, allowing them to share information, assign tasks, and communicate effectively. Whether you have multiple teams managing different parts of the network or security professionals spread across different time zones, FMC ensures that everyone is on the same page. With tools for incident tracking, event tagging, and team collaboration, FMC makes it easy to coordinate responses and decisions, no matter where your team members are located. It's like having a strategic command center where everyone can collaborate and make decisions based on the same information.

14. **Enhanced Visibility Across Multi-Cloud and Hybrid Environments.**
    As more organizations adopt multi-cloud and hybrid environments, the complexity of managing security increases. FMC is built to handle this complexity, providing unified visibility and control across both on-premises and cloud infrastructures. Whether your data lives in a private data center, a public cloud, or a hybrid of both, FMC allows you to monitor and protect all your resources from one place. It's like having a security system that's designed to look after both your house and your vacation home, ensuring that no matter where you are, you're always protected. With FMC's multi-cloud capabilities, you don't have to worry about security gaps or fragmented visibility—it provides a complete, integrated view of your entire environment.

15. **Integrating FMC with Other Cisco Security Tools: Building a Complete Security Fabric.**
    The true power of FMC lies in its ability to integrate seamlessly with other Cisco security solutions. Whether it's Cisco Umbrella, Cisco Stealthwatch, or Cisco Advanced Malware

Protection (AMP), FMC provides a central hub to manage and monitor all your security tools. This integration creates a security fabric that works together to detect, respond to, and mitigate threats across your entire network. It's like having an army of highly specialized soldiers, each with their unique skills, working together toward the same goal —network security. By bringing all these tools under one roof, FMC ensures that your defense mechanisms are coordinated, streamlined, and always working at peak efficiency.

16. **Ensuring Compliance with FMC's Regulatory Reporting.**
Compliance is a major concern for many businesses, especially those in industries like healthcare, finance, and retail. With FMC, ensuring compliance with regulatory frameworks like GDPR, HIPAA, and PCI-DSS is much easier. FMC provides built-in templates and reporting tools that make it simple to generate reports for audits, track security events, and maintain a record of your security posture. It's like having a compliance officer who's always on top of things, ensuring that your organization meets regulatory requirements without a second thought. Whether you need to provide audit reports or demonstrate your security controls, FMC makes it easy to stay compliant.

17. **Upgrading and Scaling with FMC: A Future-Proof Solution.**
As your organization grows and evolves, your security needs will change, and FMC is designed to grow with you. With its scalability and modular design, FMC can be easily upgraded and expanded to handle increased workloads or additional Firepower devices. Whether you're adding more devices, expanding your network, or adopting new technologies, FMC ensures that your security infrastructure remains flexible and adaptable. It's like having a security system that evolves with your organization, allowing you to continue strengthening your defenses as your needs change. FMC's ability to scale ensures that your network stays protected no matter how big or complex it becomes.

18. **Cloud-Based FMC: Management at Your Fingertips.**
For businesses that are embracing cloud computing, the option of using a cloud-based version of FMC offers even more flexibility and convenience. By hosting FMC in the cloud, you can manage your Firepower devices from anywhere, at any time. This cloud-based approach eliminates the need for dedicated on-premises hardware and ensures that your security infrastructure is always accessible, even if you're on the go. Whether you're working from home, traveling for business, or managing multiple global locations, cloud-based FMC gives you the freedom to monitor and manage your network's security from anywhere in the world. It's like having the keys to your security kingdom in your pocket, accessible at all times.

19. **The FMC Mobile App: Security on the Go.**
In today's world, security doesn't stop just because you're away from your desk. With the FMC mobile app, you can manage your Firepower devices and monitor network security from your smartphone or tablet. Whether you're checking alerts, reviewing incidents, or getting real-time updates, the FMC mobile app ensures that you're always connected to your network's security. It's like having the control of your security dashboard right in the palm of your hand, allowing you to make quick decisions and take immediate action

when needed. This flexibility ensures that you're never caught off guard, no matter where you are.

20. **Simplifying Security with FMC: Because Complexity Is Overrated.**
In the world of cybersecurity, simplicity can be a game-changer. FMC is designed to reduce the complexity of managing large-scale security operations by centralizing all the tools and controls in one intuitive interface. With its user-friendly design, FMC makes it easy for security professionals to manage policies, monitor events, and respond to incidents quickly and effectively. The simplicity of FMC's interface ensures that your team isn't overwhelmed by a sea of options or buried in layers of complicated menus. It's like a clean, well-organized desk where everything you need is within reach, making it easier to focus on what matters: protecting your network.

21. **Real-Time Threat Intelligence: Keeping You Ahead of Attackers.**
With FMC, you don't just react to threats—you anticipate them. Thanks to real-time threat intelligence from Cisco Talos, FMC allows you to stay ahead of the latest attack methods, vulnerabilities, and malicious actors. Talos continuously monitors the global threat landscape, feeding valuable intelligence into FMC to ensure your defenses are always up-to-date. It's like having a network of highly trained experts constantly analyzing data, finding new threats, and updating your security measures to prevent attacks. With real-time threat intelligence, FMC ensures that your security system evolves as quickly as the attackers do, keeping your defenses sharp and ready.

22. **The Total Package: FMC as the Heart of Your Network Security.**
FMC is more than just a management tool; it's the heart of your network security infrastructure. It integrates, manages, and optimizes your Firepower devices, providing real-time visibility, policy enforcement, and threat detection all from one central location. Whether you're dealing with advanced malware, phishing attacks, or network intrusions, FMC ensures that your defense systems are always working together to protect your network. Think of FMC as the conductor of an orchestra, guiding every instrument to create a harmonious, efficient, and powerful defense. With FMC at the helm, your network security is as coordinated and effective as it's ever been.

23. **FMC's Role in Proactive Defense: Being Ready for Anything.**
Network security isn't just about reacting to threats—it's about being prepared for anything that might come your way. FMC helps you build a proactive defense by continuously analyzing traffic, monitoring threats, and adjusting policies based on the latest intelligence. It's like having a coach who's constantly analyzing your opponent's moves, adjusting your strategy, and preparing you for the next attack. With FMC's proactive defense capabilities, your network is always on the offense, ensuring that potential threats are neutralized before they become full-fledged attacks.

24. **Why FMC Is the Ultimate Tool for Enterprise Security.**
For large enterprises, the stakes are high when it comes to network security. A single breach can lead to devastating consequences, which is why FMC is the ultimate tool for managing enterprise-level security. With its scalability, centralized control, and advanced threat detection capabilities, FMC ensures that enterprises are always protected, no matter

how complex or large their networks are. It provides the tools needed to manage thousands of devices, monitor network activity, and respond to incidents in real-time, making it the go-to solution for large-scale network defense. FMC is the backbone of your network security operations, ensuring your business stays safe while you focus on growing and innovating.

25. **Conclusion: FMC – The Command Center That Brings It All Together.**
In a world where network threats are constantly evolving, managing your security infrastructure requires precision, agility, and coordination. FMC is the central command that brings it all together, giving you full control over your network's defense systems. With its real-time visibility, advanced reporting, automation capabilities, and seamless integration with Cisco's other security tools, FMC ensures that your network is always protected, no matter what. Whether you're defending against the latest attack or managing a multi-cloud environment, FMC is the ultimate tool for modern network security. With FMC, your security team isn't just reacting to threats—they're always one step ahead, working smarter, faster, and more efficiently than ever before.

Chapter 9: Cisco Threat Intelligence Director (TID) – Your Network's Personal Bodyguard

1. **Introducing Cisco Threat Intelligence Director (TID): The Ultimate Digital Bodyguard.**
Imagine you're at a high-stakes event surrounded by potential threats—hackers, malware, and cybercriminals lurking in the shadows. Who do you call to keep you safe? Cisco's Threat Intelligence Director (TID), that's who. Think of TID as the bodyguard every network needs. With a sharp eye for emerging threats and the ability to react faster than a secret service agent, TID provides your network with the intelligence it needs to stay safe from harm. It's like the best bouncer in the digital world—watching, assessing, and stepping in before anything goes wrong. When a cyberattack is looming on the horizon, TID ensures your defenses are fortified, your systems are prepared, and your network stays secure. With TID, you get the peace of mind that someone (or something) is always keeping an eye out, ensuring that your data is guarded with the utmost precision and care.

2. **What Is TID: Your Intelligence Command Center.**
Cisco Threat Intelligence Director (TID) is like the central command center for all your network's security intelligence. It's where all incoming threat data converges and is then processed to provide you with the latest actionable intelligence. TID doesn't just sit around waiting for something to happen; it actively pulls in and synthesizes data from a variety of sources, including Cisco's Talos threat intelligence, to keep you updated on potential threats. If your network were a major city, TID would be the 24/7 operations room where analysts, cameras, and sensors work together to keep the streets clear of trouble. By using data from real-time attacks, TID helps you stay one step ahead of cybercriminals, responding to threats faster and more effectively. Whether it's identifying new attack vectors, recognizing suspicious activity, or preventing attacks from reaching their target, TID is your network's central hub for all things threat intelligence.

3. **Powerful Threat Data Feeds: Real-Time Intelligence at Your Fingertips.**
TID doesn't work with outdated information—it's constantly pulling in real-time threat

data from a global network of sources. This includes threat intelligence feeds from Cisco Talos, which is considered one of the best threat intelligence teams in the world. Think of it like having the world's most connected informant network, with real-time data coming from across the globe, always keeping you in the loop about emerging attacks, malware, and tactics. Every time an attack is identified somewhere in the world, TID processes this data and makes it available to your network security systems, giving you the advantage of up-to-the-minute knowledge. It's like having a digital watchtower that's always scanning the horizon for new threats. With TID's fast, reliable intelligence, your network is ready for anything that comes its way.

4. **Automatic Threat Correlation: Connecting the Dots for You.**
   A single data point might not tell you much, but when you connect the dots, a much clearer picture emerges. That's exactly what TID excels at—automatically correlating threat data to identify patterns, trends, and threats that would otherwise go unnoticed. Imagine trying to piece together a giant puzzle. Alone, the pieces seem disconnected, but once you start fitting them together, the picture becomes clear. TID does this on your behalf, instantly correlating data from multiple sources to provide a comprehensive view of what's happening on your network. This correlation helps you understand whether an incident is part of a larger, more complex attack, or if it's just a small, isolated event. By connecting the dots, TID gives you the bigger picture, ensuring that you're not just reacting to individual threats but managing broader security risks effectively.

5. **Threat Intelligence Sharing: Sharing Knowledge for a Stronger Defense.**
   In the world of cybersecurity, knowledge is power, and TID helps you share that knowledge across your security infrastructure. With TID, you can distribute actionable threat intelligence across your network, ensuring that your entire system is protected against the latest threats. Whether it's through automated updates, reports, or integration with other Cisco security products, TID ensures that every part of your network is working with the latest and most relevant threat data. It's like having a team of cyber experts constantly feeding your security system with fresh insights, ensuring that everyone is on the same page. When every part of your system is using the same high-quality intelligence, your defenses become stronger and more coordinated. Sharing knowledge isn't just helpful—it's a necessity in today's fast-paced cybersecurity landscape.

6. **Proactive Defense: Stopping Threats Before They Strike.**
   You know what they say—prevention is better than cure. TID embraces this philosophy by enabling proactive defense mechanisms across your network. By leveraging up-to-date threat intelligence, TID helps identify potential vulnerabilities and threats before they even make their move. It's like having an early warning system that detects incoming cyberattacks, allowing you to shore up your defenses before the attack even happens. TID doesn't wait for things to go wrong; it actively works to prevent them from going wrong in the first place. Whether it's blocking malicious IPs, stopping malware before it spreads, or enforcing security policies based on new threats, TID ensures that your network is always a few steps ahead of attackers.

7. **Streamlining Incident Response: Speed and Accuracy Combined.**
    When a security incident occurs, every second counts. TID streamlines your incident response process by automatically providing you with the information and context you need to act fast and accurately. Instead of wasting time trying to decipher what's going on, TID aggregates and organizes threat data, so your security team can quickly understand the scope of the problem. It's like having an incident report handed to you on a silver platter—complete with all the details, context, and suggested actions. The faster you can respond, the less damage an attack can do. TID accelerates your response time, ensuring that threats are contained quickly, minimizing their impact and keeping your network secure.

8. **Intelligence-Rich Alerts: Know What's Important.**
    Not all alerts are created equal, and when you're managing a large network, you don't have the luxury of addressing every single event. That's why TID's intelligence-rich alerts are so valuable. Instead of bombarding you with endless notifications, TID ensures that each alert is tied to high-priority threats, making sure you focus your efforts where they matter most. These alerts come with all the relevant information—such as threat type, severity, and recommended actions—so you don't waste time investigating irrelevant issues. It's like having a personal assistant who filters out the noise and delivers only the critical alerts that require your attention. This keeps your team from getting bogged down by false positives and ensures that you're always acting on the most urgent threats.

9. **Real-Time Updates: Keeping Your Defenses Sharp.**
    The world of cyber threats is constantly changing, and staying ahead of the game requires continuous updates. TID provides real-time updates to keep your threat intelligence fresh, ensuring that your defenses are always sharp and ready to face the latest challenges. As new vulnerabilities and threats emerge, TID automatically updates your network security systems with the latest data, ensuring that you're always prepared. It's like getting a constant stream of intelligence that helps you adapt to new challenges, keeping your defenses as strong as possible. With TID, your network security is never static—it's dynamic and constantly evolving to address new threats in real-time.

10. **Integration with Cisco's Security Ecosystem: A Seamless Defense.**
    When you invest in Cisco products, you're not just buying individual tools; you're building an integrated security ecosystem. TID plays a key role in this ecosystem, seamlessly integrating with other Cisco security products, such as Cisco Umbrella, Cisco Firepower, and Cisco Stealthwatch. By sharing intelligence across these products, TID helps create a unified defense strategy, ensuring that every component of your network is aligned and working together. This integration ensures that your security is both comprehensive and effective, providing a layered defense that can stop a wide range of threats. It's like having a team of specialists, each playing their part, working together to protect your network from all angles.

11. **Advanced Threat Detection: Uncovering Hidden Risks.**
    Sometimes threats don't announce themselves with a loud bang—they sneak in quietly,

hiding behind normal network activity. That's where TID's advanced threat detection capabilities come in. By analyzing traffic patterns, behaviors, and historical data, TID is able to uncover hidden risks that may not be obvious at first glance. It's like a detective piecing together clues, slowly unraveling a mystery and uncovering the attacker's next move. Whether it's detecting a slow-moving APT (Advanced Persistent Threat) or identifying suspicious lateral movement within your network, TID ensures that no threat stays hidden for long. With its deep visibility and intelligent analysis, TID can spot even the subtlest signs of an attack before it has a chance to escalate.

12. **Threat Attribution: Knowing Who's Behind the Attack.**
When an attack occurs, knowing who's behind it can be as important as stopping it. TID helps with threat attribution by correlating data across various sources to determine who's responsible for the attack. By analyzing tactics, techniques, and procedures (TTPs), TID can help identify the cybercriminals or state-sponsored actors behind the breach. It's like putting together a criminal profile—understanding their methods, objectives, and behavior patterns. With this information, your team can better prepare for future attacks, adjust your defense strategy, and take more informed actions. TID doesn't just stop the attack—it helps you understand the attackers, making it easier to anticipate their next move.

13. **Building a Stronger Defense Over Time: Learning from Each Attack.**
Every attack is an opportunity to strengthen your defenses, and TID helps you learn from each incident. By continuously analyzing threat data and incorporating lessons from previous incidents, TID helps you refine your security posture over time. It's like a seasoned fighter who learns from every bout, becoming more strategic with each round. Whether it's identifying new attack vectors, tweaking detection algorithms, or adjusting your security policies, TID ensures that your network gets stronger with each new challenge. This iterative improvement process ensures that your defenses evolve, making it harder for attackers to succeed the next time they come knocking.

14. **Visibility into Network Traffic: Understanding What's Happening.**
Understanding your network traffic is crucial to identifying and stopping threats, and TID gives you full visibility into this traffic. By analyzing incoming and outgoing traffic, TID helps you understand what's normal, what's suspicious, and what's malicious. It's like having a surveillance system that lets you watch every car entering and leaving the gates of your digital fortress. TID provides real-time analysis of network flows, highlighting unusual activity and enabling you to take action before things spiral out of control. This level of visibility helps you spot attacks that might be hidden beneath a veil of seemingly innocent traffic, allowing you to identify issues before they escalate into major problems.

15. **Streamlined Threat Mitigation: Swift Action When Needed.**
When a threat is detected, TID doesn't just report the incident—it takes immediate steps to mitigate the threat. This can involve automatically blocking malicious IPs, isolating compromised systems, or updating security rules to prevent the threat from spreading. It's like having a security guard who's always on the lookout and ready to step in when things go wrong. With TID, threat mitigation is quick and efficient, ensuring that your network

remains secure and any damage is minimized. TID allows your team to focus on strategy while it handles the heavy lifting, responding to threats swiftly and accurately.

16. **Customizable Threat Detection: Tailoring Security to Your Needs.**
Every network is unique, and so are the threats it faces. TID understands this and offers customizable threat detection capabilities to fit your specific needs. Whether you need to focus on protecting sensitive data, preventing insider threats, or blocking DDoS attacks, TID allows you to configure detection rules and policies that align with your organization's priorities. It's like having a tailor-made suit for your network security — custom-fit to provide the best protection based on your unique risk profile. This level of customization ensures that your defense strategies are as effective as possible, giving you the flexibility to focus on the areas of your network that matter most.

17. **Advanced Malware Protection (AMP): Protecting from All Angles.**
Malware can take many forms, and it's not always easy to detect. With TID's advanced malware protection, you're armed with a multi-layered defense that can catch even the most elusive threats. Whether it's viruses, ransomware, or fileless malware, TID ensures that malicious files are caught and neutralized before they can do damage. It's like having a security dog that not only sniffs out trouble but also chases it down and takes care of it. With real-time malware detection and automated responses, TID ensures that your network stays clean, reducing the risk of infection and data loss.

18. **Threat Intelligence Enrichment: Making Your Data Smarter.**
TID doesn't just process raw threat data — it enriches it, adding additional context and detail that makes the information more actionable. This enrichment might include geolocation data, threat actor profiles, or historical attack patterns that help you understand the context of the threat. It's like taking a plain piece of paper and turning it into a full report with charts, graphs, and insights that make the data easier to interpret and act on. By enriching threat intelligence, TID gives your security team the tools they need to make informed decisions quickly, improving their ability to respond to threats in real-time.

19. **Intelligent Policy Enforcement: Ensuring the Right Action is Taken.**
When TID detects a threat, it doesn't just alert you — it can also enforce policies to stop the threat in its tracks. Whether it's blocking traffic from suspicious IP addresses, quarantining infected endpoints, or enforcing stricter access controls, TID ensures that the appropriate action is taken automatically. It's like having a digital traffic cop who ensures that bad actors are kept out while allowing legitimate users to pass freely. Intelligent policy enforcement means that your security system is always acting in your best interests, responding to threats in a way that minimizes risk and keeps your network safe.

20. **Global Threat Intelligence: A Worldwide Defense.**
The world is interconnected, and so are the threats. Cisco's global threat intelligence network ensures that TID is always connected to the latest security data from around the world. Whether it's identifying the latest botnet command and control servers or detecting new phishing campaigns, TID uses global intelligence to stay ahead of the latest threats. It's like having a network of security professionals from every corner of the

globe, all working together to keep you safe. With global threat intelligence, TID gives you a comprehensive view of the threat landscape, ensuring that your defenses are always prepared for the next big attack.

21. **Actionable Insights: No More Wading Through the Data.**
Threat intelligence can be overwhelming, but TID turns that data into actionable insights that your security team can use to make informed decisions. Instead of drowning in a sea of data, TID highlights what's important, focusing on high-priority threats that require immediate attention. It's like having a well-organized filing cabinet that only shows you the most relevant documents—everything else stays hidden until you need it. By focusing on actionable insights, TID ensures that your team can take quick, effective action without getting bogged down in irrelevant details.

22. **Seamless Integration with Firepower: A Unified Defense.**
TID is designed to integrate seamlessly with Cisco Firepower devices, ensuring that threat intelligence is immediately actionable across your network security infrastructure. Whether it's applying updated threat signatures, blocking malicious IPs, or adjusting firewall policies, TID ensures that your Firepower devices are always using the latest threat data. It's like having a digital command post that ensures your security systems are working in perfect sync, with no delays or gaps in your defenses. With this seamless integration, TID and Firepower form a powerful, unified defense system that provides comprehensive protection for your entire network.

23. **Custom Alerts: Focus on What Matters.**
Not every alert requires immediate action, and TID understands that. With its customizable alert system, TID allows you to configure notifications based on the severity of the threat, the type of attack, or other relevant criteria. Whether you want to be alerted immediately about high-risk threats or receive periodic reports about minor issues, TID ensures that you're only notified about what truly matters. It's like having a personal assistant who only interrupts you when necessary, making sure you're focused on the important stuff without distractions.

24. **Intelligent Threat Blockage: Stopping Attacks in Their Tracks.**
The faster you can stop an attack, the less damage it can do. That's why TID comes equipped with intelligent threat blockage capabilities that automatically mitigate risks in real-time. When TID detects a potential threat, it can immediately block malicious traffic, quarantine infected endpoints, or even adjust network policies to prevent the threat from spreading. It's like having a quick-reacting security guard who doesn't wait for trouble to escalate—they spring into action as soon as they sense something's off. With TID, your network is always a step ahead of the attackers, ensuring that threats are stopped before they can cause significant harm.

25. **Conclusion: TID – Your Network's Ever-Vigilant Bodyguard.**
In the world of cybersecurity, staying ahead of attackers is a constant battle. Cisco's Threat Intelligence Director (TID) is your network's personal bodyguard, always vigilant, always ready to protect your assets. With its real-time threat intelligence, proactive defense mechanisms, and seamless integration with Cisco Firepower devices, TID

provides a comprehensive defense system that is always on guard. Whether you're stopping threats before they occur, responding to incidents in real-time, or learning from past attacks, TID ensures that your network is always protected. With TID by your side, you can rest easy knowing that your network's security is in the best hands—24/7, every day of the year.

Chapter 10: How to Set Up Cisco IDS/IPS Without Losing Your Mind

1. **Introduction: Welcome to the Wonderful World of IDS/IPS.**
   If you've ever tried setting up an Intrusion Detection System (IDS) or Intrusion Prevention System (IPS) on your own, you know it's a bit like assembling a piece of IKEA furniture: intimidating at first, but oddly satisfying once it's done. You've probably heard the horror stories: networks flooded with false positives, endless policy tweaks, and configurations that make you question your life choices. But fear not! Setting up Cisco's IDS/IPS doesn't have to be a mind-bending experience. With a little know-how, some patience, and a touch of humor, you can get your Cisco IDS/IPS system up and running without tearing your hair out. So, grab your favorite cup of coffee (or stronger beverage) and let's dive in, one step at a time. I promise, we'll make it as painless as possible.

2. **Step 1: Understand the Basics – IDS vs. IPS.**
   Before we start, let's clear up the difference between IDS and IPS. An IDS is like a security guard who watches everything and reports suspicious activity, but doesn't actually stop the bad guys. It gives you an alert, and then you decide what to do. IPS, on the other hand, is the bouncer who doesn't just warn you about a threat—it kicks out the troublemakers before they can even get near your network. Understanding this distinction is crucial because it will guide how you set up and configure your Cisco IDS/IPS. You need to decide whether you want the system to just warn you about threats (IDS) or proactively block them (IPS). Once you've got that down, you're on the right track.

3. **Step 2: Choose Your Hardware.**
   Cisco IDS/IPS solutions come in various flavors, and the first thing you need to do is decide which one fits your needs. Are you securing a small office network or a massive enterprise environment? Cisco offers options like the Firepower 1000 and 3000 series for different scales of deployment. Choose wisely, as the wrong hardware can lead to performance issues, or worse, security gaps. Think of it like choosing a car: a compact sedan might work for city driving, but if you're hauling a family and gear up a mountain, you'll need an SUV. Similarly, Cisco offers hardware options that will suit different environments. Consider the size of your network, your performance needs, and your budget—there's a Cisco IDS/IPS system for everyone.

4. **Step 3: Plan Your Deployment – Location, Location, Location.**
   Now that you've chosen your hardware, it's time to figure out where you're going to place your IDS/IPS in your network. The placement of your system is more important than you might think. For an IDS, you typically want to place it in a network segment where it can see all the traffic but not necessarily block it. This could be a span or mirror port on a switch or a network tap. For an IPS, on the other hand, you'll want to place it in-line with traffic, where it can actively block malicious activity. It's like setting up your

security cameras—make sure they can see all the action but don't block the flow of traffic. Getting this right will save you time and headaches down the road.

5. **Step 4: Configure Your Network Settings – It's Like Setting up Wi-Fi, But More Important.**
Once your hardware is in place, it's time to start configuring your network settings. This includes setting up the IP addresses for your IDS/IPS system, configuring default gateways, and ensuring that all the necessary interfaces are up and running. Think of it like setting up your home Wi-Fi router, but with much higher stakes. You need to make sure your system can communicate with the rest of your network and the management tools you'll be using. If you're setting up an IPS in-line, you'll also need to verify that it can communicate with your firewalls and routers to ensure traffic can be inspected and blocked when necessary. Pay attention to these settings—they're the foundation on which the rest of your setup will be built.

6. **Step 5: Connect to the Console – Time to Dive In.**
The next step is to connect to the console and start configuring the system. Depending on your Cisco model, this might involve connecting to a physical console port or accessing the system via SSH. It's like opening the door to a secret room filled with controls and buttons—don't panic! You'll be presented with a command-line interface (CLI), and while it might look intimidating, this is where the magic happens. From here, you can begin configuring your system, defining policies, and establishing rules. If you're more comfortable with a GUI, Cisco also offers a web-based management interface, which might feel more like cruising through a modern app than battling a CLI.

7. **Step 6: Set Up Your Management Interface – One Control Panel to Rule Them All.**
The management interface is where you'll be configuring most of your settings. For Cisco IDS/IPS systems, this interface is typically the Firepower Management Center (FMC). This is your cockpit, where you can monitor security events, review alerts, and manage policies. Think of FMC as the dashboard of your car: it's where you keep an eye on everything, adjust your settings, and troubleshoot when needed. Here, you'll set up your user access, define who can do what, and configure the basic settings for your network devices. It's time to make sure you've got the controls to steer your network defense ship.

8. **Step 7: Set Up the Policies – The Rules of Engagement.**
Now comes the fun part: setting up your policies. These are the rules that will dictate how your IDS/IPS system behaves. Are you going to allow certain types of traffic? Block others? The goal here is to define what is considered normal and what is not, so your system knows when to sound the alarm. It's like setting house rules for a party—what's acceptable behavior and what's not? Be careful with your thresholds—setting them too high may result in unnecessary alerts, and setting them too low may cause your system to miss real threats. The key here is finding that sweet spot, where your system is responsive without being overbearing.

9. **Step 8: Choose Your Detection Method – Signature-Based vs. Anomaly-Based.**
When setting up your policies, you'll need to decide which detection methods you want

to use. Cisco IDS/IPS systems support both signature-based detection (looking for known threats) and anomaly-based detection (looking for unusual patterns). Signature-based detection is great for stopping attacks you've already seen, but it's like putting up a "no trespassing" sign—good for preventing repeat offenders, but not great at catching new types of intruders. Anomaly-based detection, on the other hand, looks for unusual patterns in the data, which is like having a guard who's not just looking for obvious threats, but also watching for anything that seems out of place. A combination of both methods is usually the best approach, as it gives you a broader range of protection.

10. **Step 9: Enable Logging and Monitoring – You Can't Protect What You Can't See.**
The real power of your Cisco IDS/IPS system comes from the data it collects. By enabling logging and monitoring, you can keep track of every little detail about what's happening on your network. If something goes wrong, you'll have a complete trail of events to help you investigate. Just like a detective needs clues to solve a crime, your security team needs logs to identify the source of a breach or anomaly. Be sure to configure your logging settings to record the right level of detail without overwhelming your storage capacity. After all, you don't want to drown in logs, but you do want enough information to make informed decisions.

11. **Step 10: Fine-Tune Your IDS/IPS Policies – Adjusting for Accuracy.**
You're not done yet! Now it's time to fine-tune your settings. The default settings on most IDS/IPS systems are good for getting started, but they usually need some tweaking to fit your specific network environment. This is where the real art of configuring an IDS/IPS system comes into play. Look at the traffic on your network, and adjust the policies based on what you're seeing. If you're getting too many alerts, it might be time to adjust your thresholds or fine-tune the signatures. Remember, it's a marathon, not a sprint. Your IDS/IPS system will become more effective over time as you continue to adjust and learn from the events it logs.

12. **Step 11: Testing, Testing – Is Your IDS/IPS Really Working?**
You don't want to wait until an actual attack to find out if your IDS/IPS system is working. That's like waiting until your house catches fire to test your smoke detectors. Before going live, test your system with some benign traffic to see how it responds. Cisco offers tools like the Firepower Threat Defense (FTD) that let you simulate attacks without actually causing any harm. Think of it like a fire drill—you want to know that your system will react correctly when the time comes. This testing phase allows you to verify that your configuration is solid and your alerts are meaningful.

13. **Step 12: Set Up Alerts – Don't Miss the Red Flags.**
The point of an IDS/IPS is to alert you when something suspicious happens, so configuring your alert system is critical. Cisco provides several types of alerts based on severity, from informational to critical. You'll want to ensure that critical alerts are routed to the right people and that lower-priority alerts don't flood your team's inboxes. Think of it like being at a party and having your phone blow up with texts every time someone likes your Instagram post—it's a distraction. On the other hand, missing a critical alert is

like ignoring a fire alarm because you're too busy checking your phone. Strike the balance between useful alerts and noise.

14. **Step 13: Set Up Your Response – What Happens After the Alarm?**
It's one thing for your IDS/IPS to raise the alarm; it's another thing entirely for your system to know what to do once that happens. Setting up response actions for certain alerts will ensure that your system doesn't just sit there after an event. For instance, if an attack is detected, you can configure the IPS to automatically block the malicious IP or quarantine an infected host. Think of it like a well-trained security team who not only notices trouble but knows exactly how to act. The more automated your response, the faster the attack is neutralized.

15. **Step 14: Integrating with Other Tools – Teamwork Makes the Dream Work.**
Cisco IDS/IPS systems work even better when integrated with other security tools like Security Information and Event Management (SIEM) systems. By integrating with tools like Cisco Stealthwatch or Splunk, you can get a broader view of your network and improve correlation across systems. It's like having an entire security team where everyone knows their role and works together to achieve the common goal. Integration makes sure that all your defenses are aligned, and that your responses to security events are as effective as possible.

16. **Step 15: Don't Forget About Updates – Keep It Fresh.**
Your IDS/IPS system is only as good as the data it's working with. That means it's crucial to keep your signatures, policies, and software up to date. Cisco releases regular updates for both signature files and software patches, which is vital for keeping up with the latest threats. Think of it like maintaining a well-oiled machine—it needs to be periodically serviced to perform at its best. Set your system to update automatically, or at least check for updates regularly to stay ahead of attackers who are always evolving.

17. **Step 16: Avoiding False Positives – The Fine Line Between Overreacting and Underreacting.**
False positives are the annoying alarms that go off when there's no real danger. With an IDS/IPS, this can be especially frustrating, as you don't want to waste time chasing non-issues. Fine-tuning your system's thresholds and adjusting your detection methods will help minimize false positives. You're essentially teaching your system to recognize what's normal and what's not. Over time, you'll learn how your network behaves, allowing you to adjust settings for maximum accuracy. It's like learning the difference between the sound of a door creaking and someone sneaking into your house—it takes time, but you'll get it.

18. **Step 17: Documentation Is Key – Don't Skip the Paperwork.**
Once everything is configured, don't forget to document your setup. Write down the policies you've created, the thresholds you've set, and the testing you've done. It may sound like a chore, but trust me, you'll thank yourself later when you need to troubleshoot or hand the project off to someone else. Think of it like writing the instructions for a recipe—you're creating a guide to make sure others can follow the

same process, or you can refer to it in the future. Plus, documentation can help you track changes over time, especially as you tweak settings and add new features.

19. **Step 18: Test Again – Because You Can Never Be Too Sure.**
Once you've configured everything and documented it, it's time to test again. Make sure all the alerts, responses, and policies are functioning as expected. This is your final safety check before you fully deploy the system. Testing ensures that everything is in place, and you'll be able to identify any last-minute adjustments that need to be made. It's like checking your parachute before jumping out of a plane—best to be extra sure everything works.

20. **Step 19: Keep an Eye on Performance – Don't Let It Slow You Down.**
Your IDS/IPS system shouldn't slow down your network. While protecting your network is the priority, performance still matters. Make sure that the configuration you've set up doesn't introduce bottlenecks. This includes checking the throughput, latency, and resource usage of your system. You don't want to sacrifice security for speed, but you also don't want your network crawling to a halt. Regularly check your system's performance, especially after significant updates or policy changes.

21. **Step 20: Set Up Reporting – Get the Info You Need, When You Need It.**
You'll need regular reports to keep track of what's going on with your IDS/IPS. Cisco offers customizable reporting features that allow you to pull detailed logs, event summaries, and compliance reports. You can schedule these reports to be automatically generated and delivered to your inbox, ensuring that you have a constant stream of data to keep tabs on. It's like getting a health checkup for your network—a regular report that shows you where everything stands.

22. **Step 21: Tune and Improve – It's a Never-Ending Process.**
The world of cybersecurity is constantly evolving, and so are the threats. This means that your IDS/IPS configuration should be continuously tuned and improved. Regularly review your logs, update your policies, and adjust your thresholds based on the new information you're gathering. The more you fine-tune your system, the better it will perform. Don't expect to set it and forget it—network defense is an ongoing process, and your system needs to evolve as threats change.

23. **Step 22: Share Knowledge – Help Others Get It Right.**
If you've successfully set up a Cisco IDS/IPS system without losing your mind, share your knowledge with your team or colleagues. You're now a pro, and others can learn from your experience. Share your tips, your best practices, and the things that worked well (and the things that didn't) to help others avoid the same pitfalls. It's like passing along your hard-earned wisdom—because, let's face it, no one needs to reinvent the wheel.

24. **Step 23: Monitor Continuously – Stay Alert.**
Once everything is running smoothly, don't just walk away and forget about it. Continuous monitoring is essential to ensure that your IDS/IPS system is doing its job effectively. You don't need to micromanage every alert, but you do need to keep an eye

on the system's performance and security alerts regularly. Cyberattacks can happen at any time, and being proactive is the best way to stay ahead of them. Think of it like having an ever-watchful eye keeping an eye on your digital kingdom.

25. **Step 24: Relax – You've Done It!**
Congratulations—you've successfully set up your Cisco IDS/IPS system without losing your mind (or at least not completely). You've protected your network, created effective policies, and fine-tuned your system to handle the toughest threats. Now it's time to breathe easy—until the next security challenge arises, of course. But for now, sit back, relax, and enjoy the peace of mind knowing that your system is standing guard, keeping your network safe from the ever-evolving world of cyber threats.

Chapter 11: Tuning Cisco IDS/IPS – Finding the Perfect Balance Between Security and Sanity

1. **Introduction: The Balancing Act of Network Security.**
When it comes to IDS/IPS tuning, finding the perfect balance is like trying to balance a see-saw with a trampoline on one side—one wrong move and you're either overwhelmed by too many alerts or leaving gaps in your defenses. Cisco's IDS/IPS solutions are powerful tools, but without proper tuning, they can either drown you in false positives or fail to catch the real threats. Tuning your IDS/IPS system isn't just about making it more "efficient"; it's about making it smarter. The key is to set up the system so it doesn't scream "attack!" every time someone uses the printer or visit the same website twice in one day. This chapter will guide you through the art of tuning your Cisco IDS/IPS system, ensuring you have a finely tuned machine that alerts you to *real* threats without sending you to an early grave. Get ready to navigate the delicate dance of sensitivity and specificity, and, just maybe, preserve a little sanity while you're at it.

2. **Step 1: Understand the Default Settings – The Starting Point.**
Before you go fiddling with all the dials and sliders, take a moment to appreciate the default settings on your Cisco IDS/IPS. They're not perfect, but they're a solid foundation to build upon. Cisco's default configurations are designed to work for a wide variety of networks, which means they'll do a decent job for most users. However, they aren't customized to your specific network traffic, which means they'll likely flag many harmless activities as potential threats. Think of it like buying a brand new car—sure, it runs well, but you're not going to drive it across the country without checking the tire pressure, oil level, and maybe adjusting the seat. By understanding and reviewing these default settings, you'll know where to start your journey to a properly tuned system.

3. **Step 2: Define Your Environment – It's Not One-Size-Fits-All.**
Not all networks are created equal, and neither should be their IDS/IPS configurations. What works for a small business with a handful of employees won't work for a massive data center with thousands of devices. The first rule of tuning is to understand your own network's specific needs and behavior. What kind of traffic flows through your network? What are the critical systems that need extra protection? The better you understand your environment, the easier it will be to identify what normal looks like, which means you'll know when something's abnormal. Tailoring your IDS/IPS policies to fit your network is

like putting on a custom suit—it fits just right and doesn't make you look like you're wearing someone else's clothes.

4. **Step 3: Avoid the "Set-and-Forget" Mentality – Constant Monitoring is Key.**
When it comes to network security, the "set-and-forget" mentality is a dangerous one. Sure, your system may seem to be running fine, but threats evolve, and your network changes over time. Just like a plant needs watering and sunlight, your IDS/IPS system needs regular attention and fine-tuning. After your initial setup, you should be reviewing your settings and making adjustments periodically. Don't fall into the trap of thinking that once you've set up your system, you're done. It's a living, breathing entity that requires maintenance, not a static object that will defend you forever without a little TLC.

5. **Step 4: Signature Tuning – Don't Let Everything Set Off the Alarm.**
Signature-based detection is great for catching known threats, but let's be honest—if your IDS/IPS is set to alert you for every signature, you'll quickly be drowning in noise. Signature tuning is where you identify which signatures are truly necessary for your environment and disable the ones that aren't. It's like cleaning out your inbox—don't keep emails that don't serve any purpose. Review your signature rules to ensure they're aligned with the threats that are most relevant to your network. Cisco's Firepower platform offers an intuitive way to tweak signature rules, allowing you to be more selective in what gets flagged. Your system shouldn't be an overzealous watchdog; it should be a calculated, quiet observer that barks only when there's a genuine threat.

6. **Step 5: Adjust the Sensitivity – Find the Sweet Spot.**
When tuning your Cisco IDS/IPS, you're walking a fine line between sensitivity and sanity. Set the system too sensitive, and you'll end up with a flood of alerts for every single anomaly, even if it's harmless. On the flip side, set it too low, and you risk missing critical threats. It's like trying to adjust the volume on your favorite playlist—the sweet spot is somewhere between "I can't hear anything" and "my neighbors are banging on the walls." Start by adjusting the sensitivity for each category of event, such as network traffic or application behavior. Make sure the thresholds are set high enough to catch the major threats but not so low that your inbox is flooded every time someone opens a new tab in their browser.

7. **Step 6: Monitor and Adjust Policies for Specific Applications.**
Not all applications are created equal, and neither should their security policies be. Your IDS/IPS will likely flag certain applications as suspicious based on predefined signatures, but you know your network better than anyone else. Applications like email servers, VoIP, and cloud storage often generate high volumes of traffic that could trigger false positives if you're not careful. Customizing your policies for these applications can greatly reduce noise. For example, you might need to tweak policies for web servers that deal with SSL traffic or file-sharing applications that seem suspicious, but are normal for your business. By fine-tuning these application-specific settings, you ensure that the system is more accurate without overreacting.

8. **Step 7: Traffic Analysis – Know What's Normal to Spot What's Weird.**
One of the most important steps in tuning your Cisco IDS/IPS is understanding what

"normal" traffic looks like. Once you have a baseline, you can begin identifying what is abnormal. This is especially useful when adjusting your thresholds and tweaking signature rules. Start by monitoring network traffic for a few days to identify peak usage times, the most common ports and protocols in use, and typical traffic patterns. With this information, you can adjust your system to focus on the deviations from the norm — whether it's unusual traffic volumes, unexpected ports being used, or out-of-place communication between devices. Just like you wouldn't assume every person walking into a building is a criminal, you don't want your system to treat every anomaly like a potential attack.

9. **Step 8: Fine-Tune False Positives – Don't Let Alerts Eat Your Lunch.**
False positives are the bane of every network administrator's existence. They can make your IDS/IPS feel more like an annoying car alarm that goes off every time a leaf blows by. To avoid this, Cisco's IDS/IPS allows you to fine-tune the system to minimize these pesky alerts. This can be done by adjusting your thresholds, adding exceptions, and even tweaking signatures to better reflect your network environment. By carefully refining the parameters for each rule, you'll reduce the number of non-issues being flagged. Think of it as cleaning your email inbox — unsubscribing from the junk so that the important messages rise to the top. You want to avoid being desensitized to alerts due to a constant barrage of false alarms.

10. **Step 9: Customize the Event and Alert Severity Levels – Context is Everything.**
Cisco's IDS/IPS systems allow you to define the severity of various alerts. By customizing the alert severity, you can ensure that high-priority threats get the attention they deserve, while lower-priority events don't distract you. Think of it like a fire alarm that goes off when there's a candle flame and one that sounds off only when the house is on fire. By categorizing alerts into different levels — critical, high, medium, and low — you can focus on the threats that matter most while ignoring the trivial stuff. Setting up this tiered system will help you organize alerts in a way that makes them actionable without overwhelming your team with unnecessary notifications.

11. **Step 10: Establish Baseline Behavior for Effective Detection.**
Tuning your IDS/IPS requires you to establish what "normal" behavior looks like, so that the system can flag the abnormal. This means creating baseline profiles of expected network activity over time. Once your system learns what regular activity is, it can spot the unusual patterns that indicate potential threats. This can include things like a spike in traffic volume, odd communication from unknown IP addresses, or unusual packet sizes. Cisco's system allows you to track this behavior and make adjustments based on what the system learns. The more information you gather about typical traffic, the more effective your system will be at detecting and responding to potential threats.

12. **Step 11: Manage High-Traffic Areas – Don't Drown in Data.**
High-traffic areas of your network, such as web servers, email systems, or cloud storage, will inevitably generate large volumes of data. This data can quickly overwhelm your IDS/IPS if it's not managed properly. To handle this, segment your network and apply appropriate security policies to different sections. For example, you might have stricter

monitoring rules for your servers that handle sensitive data, while allowing a little more flexibility in non-critical parts of your network. This segmentation ensures that your IDS/IPS isn't flooded with irrelevant alerts and that the critical parts of your network get the most attention. It's like hiring extra security at the front door but only checking bags at the VIP section.

13. **Step 12: Don't Overload Your System with Logging.**
    Your Cisco IDS/IPS system is a powerful tool, but it can only handle so much logging without becoming sluggish. Too much logging can bog down your system and create more data to sift through. As part of your tuning process, it's essential to find a balance between logging useful information and overwhelming your system. Focus on logging events that provide value, such as suspicious traffic patterns or configuration changes, and avoid logging excessive amounts of regular traffic data. Think of it like a bouncer at a club: they don't need to keep track of every person who enters, just the ones acting out of line.

14. **Step 13: Test and Validate the Configuration – Avoid Blind Spots.**
    Once you've configured your system and tweaked the settings, it's time to test everything. You don't want to wait until an actual attack occurs to find out if your system is working properly. Use tools like Cisco's own Firepower Threat Defense to simulate traffic and attacks and see how your system responds. This allows you to spot weaknesses, validate your detection rules, and ensure that your system is accurately identifying and responding to threats. It's like conducting a fire drill to ensure that the fire alarms will work when they're needed most.

15. **Step 14: Monitor the Performance – Don't Let Security Slow You Down.**
    Security shouldn't come at the cost of performance. One of the challenges of tuning your Cisco IDS/IPS is ensuring that security doesn't slow down your network. Too many alerts or overly aggressive detection methods can introduce latency and affect network performance. Keep an eye on your system's resource utilization, especially after making changes to signature rules or detection settings. Cisco provides tools for monitoring system performance, so use them to ensure your IDS/IPS is keeping up with the traffic demands while still providing the level of protection you need. It's about striking a balance between strong security and smooth network performance.

16. **Step 15: Adjusting for New Threats – Stay Adaptable.**
    Your network environment is constantly evolving, and so are the threats. Regularly update your IDS/IPS system to keep it adaptable to new and emerging attack vectors. As new vulnerabilities are discovered, your system needs to be able to identify and block these threats effectively. Cisco's Talos threat intelligence service ensures that your system is always armed with the latest threat information. Be proactive in incorporating new intelligence and updating signatures, so your system can continue to defend against the latest attacks.

17. **Step 16: Be Aware of Resource Limitations – Don't Overload Your System.**
    While tuning your IDS/IPS for performance, it's important to keep an eye on resource limitations. Every system has its limits, and it's essential to understand what those limits

are before making adjustments. For example, over-configuring your logging settings or enabling too many inspection rules can place undue strain on your system. Monitor system resources and adjust your configuration accordingly to prevent slowdowns or missed detections. Like a runner who knows when to push forward and when to take a breath, your IDS/IPS needs to perform at its best without overexerting itself.

18. **Step 17: Don't Be Afraid to Use Vendor Support – You Don't Have to Go It Alone.**
If you're feeling overwhelmed by the tuning process, remember that Cisco's support team is there to help. With their wealth of knowledge and experience, they can assist with fine-tuning your system to ensure it's operating at peak performance. There's no shame in asking for help, especially when it comes to securing your network. Cisco also offers an extensive knowledge base, forums, and technical documentation that can help you troubleshoot and find solutions to common tuning problems. It's like hiring an experienced guide to help you navigate the wild terrain of network security.

19. **Step 18: Keep Your System Up to Date – The Cyber Threat Landscape Evolves.**
As the cyber threat landscape evolves, so should your IDS/IPS system. Regular updates are crucial to keeping your defenses sharp and your detection capabilities up-to-date. Cisco regularly releases updates to address new vulnerabilities, improve detection capabilities, and optimize system performance. Ensure that your system is configured to download and install updates automatically, or set up a routine to check for updates yourself. It's like staying current on the latest trends—what was relevant last year might not cut it today.

20. **Step 19: Stay Ahead of False Negatives – Prevention is Key.**
While false positives are the loud, annoying problems, false negatives can be just as dangerous—they're the threats that slip through the cracks undetected. One of the key aspects of tuning your Cisco IDS/IPS is ensuring that you're minimizing the risk of false negatives. By fine-tuning your signature rules, adjusting thresholds, and staying on top of new threat intelligence, you can ensure that real threats are detected and blocked. Don't let those invisible attackers get the jump on you—keep your system fine-tuned and vigilant.

21. **Step 20: Review Policies Periodically – Stay Agile.**
Just as your network evolves, so do your security policies. Over time, you may find that certain rules need tweaking, or certain threats are more prominent than others. It's important to review your IDS/IPS policies periodically to ensure they align with your changing business and security needs. Regular reviews ensure that your system stays in tune with the current threat landscape, providing optimal protection without unnecessary overhead. It's like checking in with a doctor for regular checkups—prevention and maintenance are key to long-term health.

22. **Step 21: Get Feedback from Your Team – A Collaborative Approach.**
Network security is a team effort, and getting feedback from your colleagues who use the system day in and day out can help you fine-tune your IDS/IPS even further. They might have insights into specific traffic patterns or unusual events that you might have missed. Collaboration with your security team ensures that all angles are covered and that your

tuning process is as comprehensive as possible. After all, you're not alone in this—it's a team sport, and everyone's input counts.

23. **Step 22: Tune to Your Specific Threats – Prioritize What Matters Most.**
Every network has its unique vulnerabilities and threats, so make sure you tune your IDS/IPS system to prioritize the threats that matter most to your organization. Whether it's protecting financial data, preventing DDoS attacks, or securing intellectual property, understanding your network's most valuable assets will help you tailor your security policies. Custom-tuning your system to prioritize these threats ensures that your defense is as effective as possible. It's like designing a house alarm system that's more sensitive around the valuables while not worrying too much about the front porch.

24. **Step 23: Test Again and Again – Because Perfection Takes Practice.**
Tuning your IDS/IPS system isn't a one-and-done task—it's a continuous process. After making adjustments, always test your system to ensure everything is functioning as expected. Use penetration testing tools, simulated attacks, or just daily monitoring to assess the system's effectiveness. Keep refining and tweaking, because just like network security itself, IDS/IPS tuning is an ongoing process. The more you test and adjust, the closer you'll get to finding that perfect balance between security and sanity.

25. **Conclusion: Tuning for Success – Security Doesn't Have to Be Stressful.**
By following these tuning steps, you'll be well on your way to configuring a Cisco IDS/IPS system that protects your network without overwhelming your team with false alarms or unnecessary alerts. Remember, it's all about finding the sweet spot where security meets sanity. Don't forget that your system will need periodic attention and fine-tuning to stay effective as your network and the threat landscape evolve. With a little patience and a lot of testing, you can transform your Cisco IDS/IPS system from a security monster into a well-oiled, intelligent defender that quietly watches your network and alerts you when there's real danger. Security doesn't have to be stressful—just follow the steps, keep adjusting, and you'll have a network that's safe, sound, and ready to fend off anything that comes its way.

Chapter 12: Advanced Cisco IDS/IPS Features – Going Beyond the Basics

1. **Introduction: When Basic Isn't Enough – Unlocking Advanced Features.**
The basics are great, but let's be honest: when you're serious about network security, you need more than just a basic IDS/IPS setup. Cisco's IDS/IPS solutions are like high-performance sports cars—they come with all the standard features, but once you dig deeper, you'll find that there are tons of advanced features to truly supercharge your security. Think of it as upgrading your car with a turbocharger, custom suspension, and an advanced infotainment system. In this chapter, we'll go beyond the vanilla settings and dive into the advanced features that will transform your Cisco IDS/IPS from a simple gatekeeper to a proactive, intelligent defender. Ready to push the limits of your system? Strap in—it's time to explore the power of Cisco's advanced IDS/IPS features.

2. **Step 1: Advanced Malware Protection (AMP) – Catching the Sneaky Stuff.**
Traditional IDS/IPS systems are great at detecting known threats, but the real world of

network security is a lot more complicated. Enter Advanced Malware Protection (AMP), Cisco's next-gen solution for catching everything from viruses to sophisticated ransomware. AMP works by continuously monitoring network traffic and endpoints for signs of suspicious activity, even when the malware is cleverly hiding or using new techniques to evade detection. It's like hiring a detective who's so skilled that they can spot a criminal even when they're wearing a disguise. The key here is behavior analysis —AMP doesn't just look for signatures, it watches for signs that files or traffic are behaving suspiciously. By leveraging AMP, you gain a deeper level of security that's capable of catching malware that might slip past traditional defenses.

3. **Step 2: Reputation Filtering – Knowing Who You're Dealing With.**
   One of the most overlooked advanced features in Cisco IDS/IPS is Reputation Filtering. This feature taps into Cisco's global threat intelligence network, Talos, to identify and block traffic from known bad actors before they even reach your network. Think of it as having a guest list for your network party—only allowing trusted guests and immediately ejecting anyone with a shady reputation. Reputation Filtering looks at various factors, such as IP addresses and domains that have been associated with malicious activity. By blocking traffic from these known bad sources, you prevent a significant number of attacks before they even start. With Reputation Filtering, your IDS/IPS isn't just reacting to threats; it's proactively keeping out the riff-raff.

4. **Step 3: Protocol Anomaly Detection – Spying on Suspicious Protocols.**
   Network protocols are like the languages that devices speak to one another. But what happens when someone starts speaking in code, or when a protocol starts behaving strangely? That's where Protocol Anomaly Detection comes in. This feature analyzes the behavior of network protocols, looking for anything out of the ordinary that might signal an attack. For example, if an application starts sending a higher-than-usual number of HTTP requests, it could indicate an attempted denial-of-service attack. By flagging these anomalies, Cisco's IDS/IPS can alert you to suspicious behavior even if the underlying attack isn't immediately obvious. It's like being able to detect a counterfeit passport by noticing subtle irregularities in the language, even if the document looks fine on the surface.

5. **Step 4: SSL Decryption – Seeing What's Hiding in Encrypted Traffic.**
   Encrypted traffic is a blessing for protecting data in transit, but it's also a double-edged sword for security. Cybercriminals are increasingly using encrypted channels to smuggle malicious payloads into networks. Fortunately, Cisco IDS/IPS systems can decrypt and inspect SSL/TLS traffic, allowing them to see what's hiding inside the encryption. This is like having the key to a locked box that looks completely harmless from the outside but may be hiding something dangerous. By enabling SSL decryption, you ensure that malicious traffic won't slip past your defenses just because it's encrypted. While this feature is powerful, it's essential to use it wisely and ensure it doesn't negatively impact performance, as decrypting traffic can be resource-intensive.

6. **Step 5: Intrusion Prevention with Inline Deployment – Blocking Attacks in Real Time.**

While IDS is all about detection, IPS takes it a step further by actively preventing attacks. Inline deployment is one of the most effective ways to use Cisco's IPS features because it places the system directly in the data flow, enabling it to block malicious traffic in real time. Think of it as having a security guard not just reporting on trouble but actively stopping it before it escalates. Inline IPS stops threats before they can infiltrate your network, making it one of the most proactive ways to defend against attacks. While this setup requires more careful consideration of network design and potential latency, it's well worth the effort if you want to prevent attacks from doing damage.

7. **Step 6: Advanced Custom Policies – Tailoring Detection to Your Needs.**
Every network is different, and so are its security needs. Cisco's IDS/IPS systems offer advanced custom policy creation, allowing you to define what should and shouldn't be allowed in your network. Whether you want to create exceptions for trusted IPs, block specific types of traffic, or prioritize certain applications, custom policies let you fine-tune the system to fit your organization's needs. It's like designing your own set of security rules, where you can tweak and adjust the settings until they fit perfectly. Custom policies give you the flexibility to protect your network in a way that works for your business, without relying on generic, one-size-fits-all rules.

8. **Step 7: High Availability (HA) – Keeping Your Protection Always On.**
When it comes to security, downtime is not an option. Cisco's IDS/IPS systems offer High Availability (HA) configurations, ensuring that you have continuous protection, even in the event of a hardware failure. By setting up redundant systems that work together, you ensure that if one system goes down, another immediately picks up the slack. This is like having a backup quarterback who can step in and perform just as well when the first one is injured. With HA, you reduce the risk of downtime and ensure that your network is always protected, no matter what happens behind the scenes.

9. **Step 8: Event Correlation – Connecting the Dots.**
In large environments with multiple security devices, it can be difficult to make sense of individual security events. That's where event correlation comes into play. Cisco's IDS/IPS systems can correlate events from different sources, providing a unified view of what's happening on your network. By correlating logs from various devices—such as firewalls, routers, and switches—you get a clearer picture of potential threats, helping you identify patterns that might otherwise go unnoticed. It's like connecting the dots between seemingly unrelated pieces of evidence to uncover a bigger story. This allows your security team to respond to incidents with better context and understanding, rather than reacting to individual alarms in isolation.

10. **Step 9: Customizable Alerting – Only Get the Alerts You Need.**
One of the biggest challenges of managing an IDS/IPS system is avoiding alert overload. With Cisco's customizable alerting system, you can configure which events trigger notifications, helping you avoid being bombarded with irrelevant alerts. You can set up alerts for high-severity incidents while ignoring low-level issues that don't require immediate action. It's like putting your email on "Do Not Disturb" during your work hours—you'll only get the important messages, and everything else can wait. By fine-

tuning the alert system, you ensure that your team isn't overwhelmed by noise, allowing them to focus on the threats that matter most.

11. **Step 10: Traffic Analysis and Filtering – Catching Malicious Payloads.**
Traffic analysis and filtering are two powerful features that can help you prevent attacks before they do any damage. By analyzing the traffic patterns on your network, Cisco's IDS/IPS systems can detect unusual behavior or suspicious payloads that may indicate an attack. This allows the system to filter out malicious traffic before it reaches its destination. It's like filtering out spam from your email inbox—except in this case, the spam could be a potential exploit trying to compromise your systems. By analyzing traffic in-depth, Cisco's IDS/IPS systems provide an additional layer of security, ensuring that only safe and legitimate traffic is allowed through.

12. **Step 11: Real-Time Behavioral Analysis – Detecting Zero-Day Attacks.**
Zero-day attacks are some of the most dangerous because they exploit vulnerabilities that haven't been discovered yet. Cisco's real-time behavioral analysis helps detect these attacks by looking for suspicious patterns in network traffic. Instead of relying on known attack signatures, this feature watches for deviations from expected behavior, helping to spot new and unknown threats. It's like spotting a burglar who's acting a little too suspiciously in the parking lot—before they even break into your house. By using behavioral analysis, you ensure that your system is capable of identifying threats that traditional signature-based methods might miss.

13. **Step 12: Application Layer Control – Securing the Critical Layers.**
Your network isn't just a bunch of pipes that move data around—it's made up of various layers, each with its own security needs. Cisco's IDS/IPS systems allow you to control traffic at the application layer, giving you granular control over what types of applications can communicate on your network. This includes blocking dangerous applications, managing user access, and ensuring that critical applications like email servers or web apps are properly protected. It's like building a wall around your most valuable assets, making sure only the right applications are able to get through. With application layer control, you have the flexibility to tailor your defenses to the needs of your network's critical services.

14. **Step 13: Cloud Security Integration – Defending the Hybrid Environment.**
In today's hybrid cloud environments, network security needs to extend beyond the traditional perimeter. Cisco's IDS/IPS systems offer seamless integration with cloud-based security solutions, ensuring that your network remains protected regardless of where your data resides. Whether you're managing public, private, or hybrid cloud environments, Cisco's solution ensures that your cloud assets are just as protected as your on-premises infrastructure. Think of it as building a fortress with walls that expand to the cloud, ensuring that your digital assets are defended no matter where they are. This integration allows you to monitor and control your cloud traffic, ensuring that your security policies extend across your entire infrastructure.

15. **Step 14: Network Segmentation – Defending Different Zones.**
One of the best ways to protect sensitive data and reduce attack surfaces is through

network segmentation. Cisco's IDS/IPS systems support network segmentation, allowing you to apply different security policies to different zones of your network. For example, your financial systems may need more stringent monitoring than your guest Wi-Fi network, and Cisco allows you to apply appropriate policies to each. Think of it as dividing your house into secure rooms — your personal belongings are locked away, while the guest room is much more accessible. By segmenting your network and applying tailored policies, you ensure that your most critical resources are better protected.

16. **Step 15: Cloud-Delivered Threat Intelligence – Always Stay Updated.**
One of the most powerful features of Cisco's IDS/IPS systems is its integration with cloud-delivered threat intelligence. Cisco's global threat intelligence network, Talos, continuously updates the system with new insights about emerging threats, vulnerabilities, and attack techniques. By tapping into this cloud-based intelligence, your IDS/IPS system is always equipped to handle the latest and greatest threats. It's like having an army of cybersecurity experts on call 24/7, constantly analyzing and updating your defenses. With cloud-delivered threat intelligence, your system evolves with the threat landscape, ensuring that you're always a step ahead of the attackers.

17. **Step 16: Multi-Tiered Security Policies – Layered Defense for Maximum Protection.**
When it comes to network security, more layers generally mean better protection. Cisco's IDS/IPS systems allow you to implement multi-tiered security policies that provide defense in depth. This approach ensures that your network is protected at various levels — from the perimeter to the application layer and everything in between. It's like building a security system with multiple checkpoints, ensuring that even if one layer fails, the others will still stand strong. By using multi-tiered security policies, you can create a robust and resilient defense strategy that maximizes protection while minimizing risks.

18. **Step 17: Threat Detection with Machine Learning – Let Your System Learn.**
Cisco's IDS/IPS systems aren't just rule-based; they also incorporate machine learning for smarter threat detection. By analyzing historical data and network traffic patterns, machine learning algorithms can identify emerging threats that might not yet have signatures. This approach allows your system to get better over time, learning from past incidents to recognize new attack methods. It's like having a security guard who learns from every event, getting smarter and more effective as they gain experience. With machine learning, your IDS/IPS system doesn't just react to what it's been told to look for — it anticipates potential threats based on patterns in the data.

19. **Step 18: Deeper Integration with SIEM – A Unified View of Security Events.**
For organizations that rely on Security Information and Event Management (SIEM) solutions, Cisco's IDS/IPS integrates seamlessly to provide a unified view of network security events. This integration ensures that your security team can correlate events from various sources — firewalls, routers, servers, and more — giving them a comprehensive understanding of what's happening across the network. It's like using a control tower that collects data from various airports to give air traffic controllers a complete picture of the skies. By feeding data into your SIEM, Cisco's IDS/IPS system ensures that security alerts are actionable and contextual, allowing for more effective incident response.

20. **Step 19: Application Visibility and Control – Who's Talking to Who?**
Applications are the lifeblood of modern networks, but they're also a significant source of security vulnerabilities. Cisco's IDS/IPS systems provide deep visibility into application traffic, allowing you to see exactly which applications are communicating on your network and what data they're transmitting. This visibility allows you to apply granular control over which applications are allowed to run, block malicious or unnecessary apps, and ensure that critical applications are protected. It's like having a security guard who not only watches the door but also checks what's in every package. With application visibility and control, you can ensure that your network is only running the applications that are necessary and safe.

21. **Step 20: Context-Aware Security – Smarter Detection Based on Context.**
Context-aware security is a next-gen approach that makes your Cisco IDS/IPS system smarter by taking into account not just traffic patterns, but the context in which the traffic is happening. For example, an unusual file transfer might be completely normal if it's between two trusted servers, but highly suspicious if it's from an unrecognized device. Context-aware security looks at this type of information, ensuring that alerts are based on a comprehensive understanding of the network environment. It's like having a security guard who knows the regulars and can tell when someone unfamiliar is behaving oddly. By using contextual data, you can ensure that your system only raises alarms when something really out of the ordinary is going on.

22. **Step 21: Customizable Logging and Reporting – Your Network, Your Rules.**
Logs and reports are essential for tracking security events, but they can quickly become overwhelming if not customized properly. Cisco's IDS/IPS solutions allow you to create custom logs and reports that focus on what matters most to your network. Whether you need to report on compliance, investigate specific incidents, or get an overview of network activity, Cisco lets you tailor the output to meet your specific needs. It's like having a personal assistant who sorts through all the clutter to present you only the most relevant and actionable information. Customizable logging and reporting ensure that your network security is both effective and manageable, providing you with the insight you need when you need it.

23. **Step 22: End-User and Device Profiling – Knowing Who's Who.**
Identifying which users and devices are accessing your network is crucial for ensuring security. Cisco's IDS/IPS systems offer end-user and device profiling capabilities, allowing you to see exactly who is connecting to your network and what they're doing. This profiling ensures that only authorized users and devices are granted access to sensitive resources. It's like having a VIP list for your network—if someone shows up who's not on the list, they're immediately flagged for review. With this feature, you gain better visibility into your network's activity and can ensure that your most valuable resources are protected.

24. **Step 23: Advanced Threat Detection and Blocking – Proactive, Not Reactive.**
Cisco's advanced threat detection and blocking capabilities go beyond simple signature matching, offering proactive protection against sophisticated attacks. By analyzing traffic

behavior, identifying unusual patterns, and leveraging machine learning, Cisco's IDS/IPS systems can detect and block even the most advanced threats before they cause damage. This proactive approach helps you stay one step ahead of attackers, rather than merely reacting to threats after they've already penetrated your defenses. It's like having a guard dog that's trained to detect threats before they even enter your property.

25. **Conclusion: Your Next-Level IDS/IPS System – Be Prepared for Anything.**
By leveraging these advanced features, you'll transform your Cisco IDS/IPS system from a simple reactive tool into a proactive, intelligent defender of your network. Whether it's catching malware with AMP, blocking known bad actors with Reputation Filtering, or utilizing machine learning to detect zero-day attacks, these advanced features provide an extra layer of security that's tailored to your network's needs. With a little tweaking and some strategic implementation, you can ensure that your network stays protected, your alerts are actionable, and your performance is optimized. As you move beyond the basics, you'll unlock the full potential of your Cisco IDS/IPS system—making it smarter, faster, and more capable of defending against the ever-evolving world of cyber threats.

Chapter 13: Real-World Scenarios – When Hackers Show Up, and What Cisco Did About It

1. **Introduction: The Worst Happens—Here's How Cisco Handles It.**
Picture this: it's a quiet Friday afternoon, you're sipping your coffee, and then—bam!— an alert hits your screen: "Suspicious activity detected." Your heart drops, your pulse spikes, and you start frantically Googling "What to do when hackers invade." This chapter is about those moments when your network is under attack, and how Cisco's IDS/ IPS systems swoop in like superheroes to save the day. With real-world examples, we'll show how Cisco's security solutions handle these situations, keeping your network safe from harm and—let's be honest—saving your sanity in the process. From DDoS attacks to advanced persistent threats (APTs), Cisco's systems have been put to the test, and here's how they've come out on top. So buckle up, because when the hackers show up, Cisco is always ready for action.

2. **Step 1: The Great DDoS Attack – The Flood of Traffic That Never Ends.**
It's the middle of the night, and your e-commerce site is under siege. A distributed denial-of-service (DDoS) attack floods your servers with millions of requests, and your website crashes faster than a toddler on a sugar rush. If you're running a Cisco IDS/IPS system, however, things don't have to go south in a hurry. Cisco's DDoS mitigation capabilities spring into action, identifying the malicious traffic and filtering out the bad requests. It's like a bouncer at the door turning away party crashers while letting in the VIPs. As the DDoS flood continues, Cisco's system isolates the malicious traffic without disrupting the legitimate user connections. Within moments, your servers are back to business, and the attackers are left scratching their heads, wondering why their attack didn't succeed. Thanks to Cisco, your network weathered the storm and you still have time for that second cup of coffee.

3. **Step 2: The Phishing Scheme – When Hackers Try to Trick Your Users.**
A phishing attack hits your organization, and suddenly your employees are getting

suspicious emails with attachments promising "urgent updates." They're all too eager to click, and some of them do. While the attackers try to sneak malware into your network via these bogus emails, Cisco's Advanced Malware Protection (AMP) is on the case. AMP doesn't just rely on signatures to catch the bad guys—it uses behavior analysis to detect suspicious file activity and malicious payloads. It's like having a guard dog that doesn't bark at every squirrel but knows exactly when something dangerous is lurking. The minute one of the employees downloads the malicious attachment, Cisco's IDS/IPS system isolates the infected machine and prevents it from spreading. Cisco's real-time threat intelligence, powered by Talos, updates the system instantly, ensuring that no similar attack slips through. The result? A botched phishing attack and a cybersecurity team high-fiving because they didn't have to clean up the mess.

4. **Step 3: The Insider Threat – When the Enemy Is Within.**
   You've always worried about external threats, but what about the insider threat? You've just hired a new employee who, for reasons unknown, is trying to download sensitive company files. Cisco's IDS/IPS system doesn't just sit back and watch; it's actively monitoring the behavior of network traffic and user activity. As the employee starts accessing restricted data, the system's anomaly-based detection flags the behavior as suspicious. It's like having a watchful eye on everyone, even the ones who are supposed to be trustworthy. Cisco's behavior analytics reveal that the user's actions are unusual, and the IPS immediately quarantines the machine from the rest of the network. While the employee's attempt to breach the network goes unnoticed by most, Cisco's system acts swiftly, preventing any potential damage. And just like that, the insider threat is neutralized without a single file being leaked. It's a reminder that while you can't control human behavior, you can certainly control what happens to your data.

5. **Step 4: The Ransomware Attack – When Your Files Are Held Hostage.**
   Ransomware has become one of the most feared attacks in recent years, and for good reason—hackers lock up your files and demand payment for the decryption key. But don't panic—Cisco's AMP is ready for this very scenario. As the malware tries to encrypt your files, AMP's file behavior analysis kicks in, detecting the suspicious activity in real-time. It's like trying to smuggle something past an x-ray scanner—it just doesn't work. Cisco's system immediately blocks the ransomware, stopping it dead in its tracks before it can do any damage. Even if the ransomware tries to hide behind legitimate files, Cisco's machine learning-powered detection recognizes the abnormal behavior and neutralizes it. With the system in place, the attackers are left with nothing, and your files are untouched, ready to be restored. The only thing left to do? Report the attack to your legal team, who'll be pleased to know that no ransom will be paid today.

6. **Step 5: The Advanced Persistent Threat (APT) – The Sneaky Intruder.**
   Advanced Persistent Threats (APTs) are like cyber ninjas—silent, stealthy, and incredibly difficult to detect. A hacker infiltrates your network and quietly moves from one system to another, gathering information over time without triggering alarms. Enter Cisco's machine learning-powered anomaly detection. As the APT actor begins moving laterally within the network, Cisco's IDS/IPS is watching closely for any unusual behavior. Whether it's a sudden spike in data traffic, strange login patterns, or accessing

unauthorized systems, Cisco's system flags the activity. It's like trying to sneak through a laser grid in a heist movie — Cisco's system sees it all. With the attack halted before it gains any traction, the threat actor is blocked, and your network is once again safe. The APT might have been sophisticated, but Cisco's intelligence was even more sophisticated.

7. **Step 6: The Zero-Day Exploit – When the Hackers Exploit What You Don't Know.**
Zero-day vulnerabilities are a nightmare because they exploit unknown weaknesses in software before anyone knows they exist. This is where Cisco's continuous threat intelligence updates come in handy. Talos, Cisco's global threat intelligence network, works around the clock to identify new vulnerabilities as they're discovered. When a new zero-day exploit attempts to infiltrate your network, Cisco's IPS is already equipped with the latest signatures and behavioral patterns to block it. Think of it like the cybersecurity equivalent of keeping a secret weapon in reserve — when the unknown threat shows up, your system is ready. In real-time, Cisco's system blocks the attack before it even reaches your network, thanks to the proactive intelligence it constantly receives. The hackers are left frustrated, knowing their zero-day exploit is no longer effective, and your network remains secure.

8. **Step 7: The SQL Injection Attack – When Hackers Try to Wriggle In.**
SQL injection attacks are the classic "hacker trick" where malicious SQL code is inserted into a database query to gain unauthorized access. While this attack method might seem like an old-school play, Cisco's IDS/IPS system has evolved to spot these types of threats before they wreak havoc. By inspecting traffic and queries, the system can identify suspicious or malicious SQL commands and block them immediately. It's like having a bouncer who knows every trick in the book and won't let any rogue party crashers through. When the hacker tries to inject harmful code into the database, Cisco's IPS spots the anomaly and immediately blocks the attempt. Thanks to Cisco, the hacker's plan is foiled, and your database is safe and sound. And, of course, the best part is that you didn't even need to lift a finger.

9. **Step 8: The Botnet Command and Control – When Hackers Make Their Move.**
Botnet attacks involve a group of compromised computers controlled remotely by an attacker. If a botnet tries to contact its command and control server, Cisco's Reputation Filtering and Threat Intelligence services immediately spring into action. Using Talos, Cisco's threat intelligence system, it identifies the malicious IP addresses associated with botnets and blocks them before any further damage can be done. It's like being able to intercept a suspicious package before it reaches its destination — no need to wait for the damage to occur. The attackers, hoping to command their army of bots, are left stranded, unable to communicate with their compromised machines. Cisco's proactive defense ensures that botnet traffic never makes it into your network, and your infrastructure remains unscathed.

10. **Step 9: The DDoS Amplification Attack – The Attackers Try to Use Your Systems Against You.**
A DDoS amplification attack is a sneaky trick where attackers send small queries to

public servers and amplify the traffic to overwhelm the target. Cisco's IDS/IPS system stops this cold by identifying malicious traffic patterns in real time. With its traffic filtering and anomaly detection features, the system isolates malicious traffic and prevents your servers from becoming the unwitting tools of the attackers. It's like someone trying to use your home as a base to launch a water balloon fight, and you catch them before they can get started. Cisco's system keeps your servers clean and safe, ensuring they're not part of the botnet army. As the attackers try to amplify their efforts, Cisco's defenses hold strong, keeping your network operational and the bad guys frustrated.

11. **Step 10: The Ransomware Phishing Combo – Double the Trouble, Double the Defense.**

    Imagine this: a ransomware attack is combined with phishing emails targeting your employees. If left unchecked, this could lead to both encrypted files and stolen login credentials. But with Cisco's AMP for Endpoints and its comprehensive network monitoring, both threats are detected and stopped before they gain traction. As the phishing email arrives, AMP analyzes the attachment for any suspicious activity. If the malware tries to execute, AMP immediately isolates the infected machine. Simultaneously, Cisco's IDS/IPS system detects any attempts to encrypt files or execute malicious scripts, blocking them before they can lock up your valuable data. The bad guys may have had two tricks up their sleeves, but Cisco was ready with two defenses.

12. **Step 11: The Brute Force Attack – When Hackers Keep Trying Until They Get In.**

    Brute force attacks are all about persistence—the attacker uses automated tools to try countless combinations of usernames and passwords to gain unauthorized access. Cisco's IDS/IPS system is constantly monitoring for these types of attacks and can quickly identify the telltale signs of a brute force attempt. As the system sees repeated login failures from the same source, it can automatically lock down the compromised account or block the attacking IP address. It's like having a guard who spots someone trying to sneak into a building by repeatedly trying different keys and promptly calls security. With Cisco's proactive approach, the brute force attack is halted before it can cause any damage, and the attacker is left with nothing but frustration.

13. **Step 12: The Man-in-the-Middle Attack – When Hackers Listen in on Your Conversations.**

    A man-in-the-middle (MitM) attack occurs when a hacker secretly intercepts and relays communications between two parties, often without either party knowing. Cisco's IDS/IPS can detect suspicious traffic patterns that indicate a MitM attack in progress, especially when SSL/TLS decryption is in play. If malicious actors try to intercept encrypted communications, Cisco's system flags the abnormal decryption process and blocks the malicious connection. It's like intercepting a phone call and realizing that the conversation was being listened to by a hacker—you stop the eavesdropper in their tracks. With Cisco's security tools, your sensitive communications remain private, even when the attacker thinks they've found a way in.

14. **Step 13: The Credential Stuffing Attack – When Hackers Try Your Passwords Again and Again.**

Credential stuffing attacks rely on the fact that people often reuse passwords across multiple sites. The attackers use a list of stolen credentials and try them across numerous sites and services. Cisco's IDS/IPS system detects abnormal login attempts across different platforms and services, flagging any suspicious patterns. It's like a bank noticing that someone is trying to use the same stolen credit card at multiple ATMs across the city. The system can immediately block the malicious attempts, stopping the attacker before they can do any damage. Cisco's real-time monitoring ensures that even if your employees are reusing passwords, the attackers won't be able to access your critical systems.

15. **Step 14: The Cross-Site Scripting (XSS) Attack – When Hackers Try to Inject Malicious Scripts.**
Cross-Site Scripting (XSS) attacks occur when hackers inject malicious scripts into web pages viewed by other users. Cisco's IDS/IPS systems can detect malicious scripts by analyzing web traffic patterns and looking for common signs of XSS attacks. If a hacker tries to inject a script into a web page, Cisco's system can identify the suspicious payload and block the attack before it executes. It's like having a security guard who notices a strange package hidden in plain sight and quickly removes it before anyone else gets near it. By stopping XSS attacks in their tracks, Cisco ensures that your website's users are protected from the malicious code and your site remains secure.

16. **Step 15: The DNS Tunneling Attack – When Hackers Use DNS to Sneak In.**
DNS tunneling is a sneaky attack where hackers use the DNS protocol to tunnel malicious traffic into your network. Cisco's IDS/IPS systems are designed to detect abnormal DNS behavior, such as unusually large query sizes or requests to suspicious domains. This feature ensures that hackers can't use DNS as a backdoor into your network. It's like noticing a person trying to sneak into a building through an air vent instead of the front door—you stop them before they even make it inside. With Cisco's DNS tunneling detection, you block this tactic at the door, keeping your network secure from hidden attacks.

17. **Step 16: The API Abuse Attack – When Hackers Exploit Your Public Interfaces.**
APIs (Application Programming Interfaces) are essential for modern applications, but they can also be a target for abuse. Cisco's IDS/IPS systems monitor API traffic for signs of abuse, such as excessive requests or attempts to exploit vulnerabilities in the API itself. If a hacker tries to overload or manipulate your public-facing API, Cisco's system blocks the malicious traffic before it can exploit the vulnerability. It's like a bouncer at a club who only lets in people with legitimate invitations—no matter how slick the hacker's moves are, they can't get past Cisco's defenses. With advanced API protection, your interfaces stay secure, and your systems remain protected from unwanted access.

18. **Step 17: The Zero-Day Phishing Combo – When the Attackers Try to Use New Techniques.**
Hackers often combine zero-day exploits with phishing techniques to increase their chances of success. Cisco's systems are equipped with both signature-based and anomaly-based detection to stop this type of attack before it can cause damage. If a

phishing email tries to deliver a zero-day exploit, Cisco's AMP will recognize the suspicious behavior and block the malware before it can execute. Meanwhile, the IPS will stop any malicious traffic trying to reach your servers. The attackers are left scratching their heads while your systems stay intact and your data stays safe.

19. **Step 18: The Remote Desktop Protocol (RDP) Bruteforce – When Hackers Try to Guess Your RDP Password.**
RDP brute force attacks are common when attackers try to gain unauthorized access to remote machines. Cisco's IDS/IPS system monitors login attempts and flags excessive or failed RDP login attempts. If the system detects a potential brute force attack, it can automatically block the offending IP address, preventing any further attempts. This proactive defense is like having a highly observant doorman who quickly notices when someone's trying to sneak in by guessing the code and stops them in their tracks. With Cisco, your RDP connections are safe from unauthorized access, and the attackers are left out in the cold.

20. **Step 19: The Malicious Flash Drive – When Hackers Try to Sneak In via USB.**
USB-based attacks are still a threat, with hackers trying to sneak malware onto your network via infected flash drives. Cisco's AMP for Endpoints offers a solution by continuously scanning files on USB drives as they're inserted into your systems. If the system detects any suspicious files or malware on the drive, it immediately isolates the infected device and prevents the malicious software from executing. It's like having a guard dog that sniffs out anything toxic and immediately takes action. With Cisco's endpoint protection, you can confidently plug in your devices without worrying about bringing malware into your network.

21. **Step 20: The Drive-By Download – When Hackers Try to Slip Malicious Code onto Your Devices.**
Drive-by downloads are a sneaky way for hackers to deliver malware through seemingly innocent websites. Cisco's AMP detects suspicious file downloads and stops them before they can execute, blocking the malicious code in its tracks. It's like walking into a store, seeing a bunch of suspicious-looking packages, and refusing to let them past the door. With Cisco's protection, your users won't unknowingly download malware while browsing the web. Whether they're on a corporate network or using mobile devices, Cisco's system ensures that drive-by downloads never reach their destination.

22. **Step 21: The Social Engineering Attack – When Hackers Try to Trick Your Users.**
Social engineering is all about manipulating people into giving up sensitive information or clicking on malicious links. Cisco's IDS/IPS system may not be able to stop every human error, but it can help by flagging unusual behavior patterns that suggest an attack is in progress. For example, if users suddenly start clicking on suspicious links in emails, the system can block malicious sites and prevent malware from being downloaded. It's like a well-trained security guard who can spot a scam artist from a mile away and steps in before they can make their pitch. Cisco's advanced analytics help spot the subtle signs of social engineering before it turns into a major breach.

23. **Step 22: The Spoofing Attack – When Hackers Try to Fake Their Identity.**
Spoofing attacks involve hackers impersonating legitimate systems or users to gain unauthorized access. Cisco's system uses advanced IP and MAC address filtering to detect and block spoofed traffic, ensuring that only legitimate devices can access your network. It's like catching a thief trying to use a fake ID to get into a VIP club—you stop them before they can make their move. With Cisco's security features, spoofing attempts are quickly identified and blocked, ensuring that only verified traffic gets through to your systems.

24. **Step 23: The Cross-Site Request Forgery (CSRF) Attack – When Hackers Try to Trick Your Users into Doing Their Bidding.**
CSRF attacks manipulate authenticated users into performing unwanted actions on websites. Cisco's IDS/IPS system can detect these attacks by analyzing the HTTP requests for any suspicious patterns. If an attacker tries to send a forged request from a trusted user's browser, Cisco's system blocks the malicious action. It's like noticing someone trying to send a fake order from a trusted customer and stopping it before the request goes through. By stopping CSRF attacks early, Cisco ensures that your web applications remain secure and your users are protected.

25. **Conclusion: Cisco to the Rescue – Protecting Your Network, One Attack at a Time.**
Real-world cyberattacks can be daunting, but with Cisco's IDS/IPS system, you're never alone. Whether it's a DDoS attack, a phishing scam, or a sophisticated APT, Cisco's advanced features ensure that your network is ready to handle anything that comes its way. Through proactive detection, machine learning, real-time updates, and deep intelligence from Talos, Cisco provides the comprehensive defense your network needs. So, next time the hackers come knocking, you can rest easy knowing that Cisco is on the job, keeping your systems safe and your data secure. No attack is too big, and no threat is too sophisticated for Cisco's IDS/IPS system to handle—because when the hackers show up, Cisco is always ready to fight back.

Chapter 14: The Future of Cisco IDS/IPS – Riding the Waves of Emerging Threats

1. **Introduction: The Cybersecurity Ocean – Where the Waves Never Stop.**
The world of cybersecurity is a vast ocean. The waves of emerging threats are constant, and the tide of technology keeps shifting beneath our feet. If you're in charge of protecting your network, you're like a surfer, paddling out to ride the next big wave of security challenges. But how do you stay balanced? How do you keep riding those waves and avoid wiping out? The answer: Cisco's IDS/IPS solutions. As we look to the future, Cisco's technology continues to evolve, adapting to the new and ever-changing landscape of cyber threats. With new attacks on the rise, Cisco is constantly refining its capabilities to ensure that you're ready for anything. In this chapter, we'll dive into how Cisco is preparing for the future of cybersecurity, ensuring that your defenses stay ahead of the curve. So grab your surfboard—we're about to ride the wave of emerging threats together.

2. **Step 1: Machine Learning – The Brain Behind the Shield.**
Machine learning (ML) is one of the most exciting developments in the world of

cybersecurity. Instead of relying solely on pre-programmed signatures, Cisco's IDS/IPS systems will increasingly use machine learning to detect and respond to threats. ML algorithms can analyze traffic patterns and learn from past attacks, getting smarter over time. It's like having a bodyguard who becomes more skilled and intuitive with each encounter. As Cisco incorporates more ML into its IDS/IPS solutions, the system will be able to detect even the most sophisticated attacks, including zero-day exploits and novel malware strains. Think of it as a security system that's constantly evolving, learning from the latest threats, and adapting its defenses accordingly. As ML technology continues to advance, Cisco's IDS/IPS systems will be able to offer even more precise and automated threat detection.

3. **Step 2: AI-Powered Threat Intelligence – Cisco's Crystal Ball.**
   Artificial Intelligence (AI) is the future of cybersecurity, and Cisco is already harnessing AI to enhance its IDS/IPS systems. With AI-powered threat intelligence, Cisco's systems can analyze vast amounts of data in real-time, identifying patterns that humans might miss. It's like having a crystal ball that allows Cisco to predict potential threats before they even occur. AI isn't just about reacting to known threats — it's about anticipating the next wave of attacks and preparing for them. By integrating AI with Cisco's existing threat intelligence network, Talos, the system can continuously update its defenses based on the latest global threat data. As cybercriminals become more sophisticated, AI ensures that Cisco's IDS/IPS systems stay one step ahead, preventing attacks before they even begin. The future of cybersecurity is proactive, not reactive — and Cisco is leading the charge.

4. **Step 3: Cloud Security – Expanding the Horizon.**
   As businesses continue to migrate to the cloud, the scope of cybersecurity needs to evolve. Traditional on-premises security systems were built to protect physical infrastructures, but now, with data and applications scattered across the cloud, protection needs to be more dynamic and distributed. Cisco's IDS/IPS systems are already designed to integrate with cloud environments, providing comprehensive protection across multi-cloud and hybrid setups. The future of Cisco IDS/IPS will see even more focus on securing cloud-based infrastructures, offering real-time monitoring and protection across public, private, and hybrid clouds. With this level of integration, Cisco ensures that your network security isn't limited to one location — it spans across your entire digital ecosystem, from on-prem servers to the cloud and beyond. As businesses embrace the flexibility and scalability of the cloud, Cisco will continue to evolve its IDS/IPS solutions to match, offering continuous, dynamic protection that adapts to your needs.

5. **Step 4: Automated Threat Response – The Speed of Light.**
   One of the biggest challenges in cybersecurity is the speed at which attacks can occur. A hacker can breach a network in mere seconds, but responding to that attack can take hours, sometimes days. That's where automation comes in. In the future, Cisco IDS/IPS systems will increasingly rely on automated threat response, enabling them to react to attacks at lightning speed. Automated responses can range from blocking malicious IPs to isolating infected devices and even adjusting security policies in real-time. The goal is to eliminate the delay between detection and response, ensuring that your defenses are as

fast as the threats trying to breach them. By automating these processes, Cisco ensures that your security team isn't bogged down with manual interventions and can focus on strategic tasks, while the system handles the grunt work.

6. **Step 5: Threat Hunting – Proactively Searching for Trouble.**
    While automated defenses are essential, sometimes you need a human touch to truly uncover the most advanced threats. Enter threat hunting—an increasingly important tool in the cybersecurity world. Cisco's IDS/IPS systems are evolving to not just respond to attacks but to proactively seek out hidden threats. Think of it as a security expert going on the offensive, searching for signs of intrusion or exploitation deep within your network. By combining real-time monitoring with machine learning and AI-driven analytics, Cisco's systems will enable security teams to hunt down potential threats before they escalate into full-blown attacks. This proactive approach gives businesses a way to stay ahead of cybercriminals, turning the tables and making the hackers the ones who have to worry.

7. **Step 6: Next-Generation Firewall Integration – Two Defenders, One Mission.**
    The IDS/IPS system is a critical part of your network security, but it doesn't work in isolation. In the future, Cisco IDS/IPS solutions will work even more closely with next-generation firewalls (NGFWs) to provide an integrated, layered defense. By combining the strengths of both systems, businesses can create a unified, end-to-end security solution that provides deeper insights and faster response times. Next-gen firewalls can block malicious traffic, while IDS/IPS systems can detect and prevent attacks in real time. This integrated approach ensures that your defenses are more robust and that threats don't slip through the cracks. It's like having a two-pronged defense strategy—both stopping attacks at different stages but working seamlessly together.

8. **Step 7: Predictive Analytics – Looking Into the Future of Cybersecurity.**
    Predictive analytics is the future of cybersecurity, and Cisco is already integrating it into its IDS/IPS systems. By analyzing historical attack data and patterns, Cisco's system can predict future threats, identifying potential vulnerabilities before they're exploited. It's like having a crystal ball for your network—by seeing where future threats might come from, you can proactively address those risks. Predictive analytics uses data mining, machine learning, and statistical algorithms to make educated predictions about potential threats. This future-focused approach enables businesses to be prepared for attacks before they even happen, drastically reducing the risk of breaches and downtime.

9. **Step 8: Improved User and Entity Behavior Analytics (UEBA) – Understanding the Who, What, and Why.**
    User and Entity Behavior Analytics (UEBA) is an advanced feature that focuses on analyzing how users and devices behave within your network. This data helps Cisco's IDS/IPS systems recognize when something unusual occurs. As cybercriminals often exploit normal user behaviors, UEBA can spot abnormal activity, such as someone trying to access data they shouldn't be, or a device suddenly acting out of character. As Cisco incorporates more sophisticated UEBA into its IDS/IPS systems, it will be able to detect subtle, evolving threats that might otherwise go unnoticed. It's like having a watchdog

that's not just guarding the door, but also understanding the patterns of everyone inside. By monitoring how entities behave, Cisco can catch the bad guys early, preventing breaches before they get too far.

10. **Step 9: Enhanced Mobile Device Security – Securing the New Frontier.**
Mobile devices are the new perimeter of the modern network. With so many employees working remotely and using mobile devices to access corporate data, it's essential to include them in your security strategy. Cisco IDS/IPS systems will continue to evolve to monitor and protect mobile traffic, ensuring that devices—whether on the corporate network or accessing remotely—are secure. By integrating mobile device security into its overall IDS/IPS solution, Cisco provides comprehensive protection that covers all entry points, not just the traditional desktop. As mobile devices become an even larger part of business operations, Cisco will ensure they're always protected, regardless of where they connect from.

11. **Step 10: Cloud-Native IDS/IPS – Defending the Future of the Cloud.**
Cloud-native technologies are becoming more and more prevalent, and traditional security systems are struggling to keep up. Cisco's IDS/IPS solutions are moving toward becoming fully cloud-native, providing real-time, scalable protection for workloads running in the cloud. This approach will allow businesses to protect cloud-based applications, databases, and services with the same level of security they have on-premises. With cloud-native IDS/IPS, Cisco can offer a defense that's just as flexible and scalable as the cloud itself. This ensures that as businesses scale their cloud infrastructures, their security can scale with them. It's the perfect solution for the modern, cloud-first world.

12. **Step 11: Distributed Denial-of-Service (DDoS) Defense – Always On, Always Ready.**
As DDoS attacks become more frequent and sophisticated, Cisco's IDS/IPS systems will increasingly focus on real-time DDoS defense. Cisco's technology already offers some of the best DDoS mitigation tools available, but future advancements will allow for even faster, more effective responses. Real-time traffic analysis, combined with machine learning and threat intelligence from Talos, will enable Cisco's IDS/IPS to recognize and mitigate DDoS attacks in the early stages. By utilizing a combination of cloud-based and on-premises protections, Cisco ensures that your network will remain operational even during the most massive DDoS attacks. Think of it as having a moat that automatically fills with water the moment a threat approaches, ensuring your digital castle remains safe.

13. **Step 12: Expanded Threat Intelligence Integration – Staying Ahead of the Game.**
Cisco has always been a leader in threat intelligence, but as threats become more complex, the integration of intelligence into IDS/IPS systems will become even more critical. Cisco's Talos threat intelligence network will provide even more robust, real-time threat data to power IDS/IPS defenses. By integrating this intelligence into the system's detection and response capabilities, Cisco will ensure that every new threat is caught before it can do any damage. It's like having an army of cybersecurity experts scanning the horizon, constantly providing your system with fresh, actionable intelligence. With

the future of IDS/IPS fully integrated with global threat intelligence, you can rest assured that your defenses will always be on point.

Chapter 14: The Future of Cisco IDS/IPS – Riding the Waves of Emerging Threats

1. **Introduction: The Cybersecurity Ocean – Where the Waves Never Stop.**
   In the vast ocean of cybersecurity, new waves of threats are constantly forming, rising, and crashing down on organizations everywhere. It's like trying to surf during a storm—you're always battling against unpredictable forces. As the surf gets more intense, so do the threats to your network. But fear not—Cisco's IDS/IPS systems are your surfboard, designed to help you ride the waves of these emerging threats with agility and precision. The world of cyberattacks is constantly changing, and as new technologies emerge, so do new attack methods. Hackers are creative, persistent, and always on the lookout for vulnerabilities. The real question is: how can your network defense stay ahead of these ever-evolving threats? Well, that's where Cisco IDS/IPS comes in. By constantly evolving and adapting, Cisco ensures that your network stays protected from even the most dangerous and unpredictable waves in the world of cybersecurity.

2. **Step 1: Machine Learning – The Brain Behind the Shield.**
   Machine learning (ML) is like the secret sauce in the future of cybersecurity. Cisco's IDS/IPS solutions are already leveraging the power of ML to enhance threat detection and response. Unlike traditional systems that rely solely on predefined signatures, ML can analyze network behavior and learn from past attacks. As Cisco's system encounters new threats, it gets smarter, recognizing patterns that were previously undetectable. It's like having a security guard who learns from every incident and gets better at spotting the bad guys over time. As the world of cyber threats continues to evolve, ML allows Cisco's systems to adapt and recognize new forms of attack without needing to be manually updated every time. The system can predict potential risks based on historical data and current network activity, providing you with a proactive defense. With machine learning in play, Cisco's IDS/IPS solutions offer a level of intelligence that traditional systems can only dream of.

3. **Step 2: AI-Powered Threat Intelligence – Cisco's Crystal Ball.**
   Artificial Intelligence (AI) is another cornerstone of Cisco's IDS/IPS future. Think of AI as the psychic that can predict the next big cybersecurity storm. Cisco is leveraging AI to enhance its real-time threat intelligence, offering insights into potential risks before they even materialize. By integrating AI into its system, Cisco can quickly analyze vast amounts of threat data from around the globe, making predictions about emerging attacks. This ensures that your system is constantly aware of the latest threats, adjusting its defenses accordingly. It's like having a global network of cybersecurity experts working 24/7, analyzing data from every corner of the internet and feeding it back to your system. As cybercriminals continue to become more sophisticated, AI-powered threat intelligence provides the crucial edge in outsmarting them. With AI at the helm, Cisco ensures that your defenses are more responsive, agile, and ready for anything the future throws at you.

4. **Step 3: Cloud Security – Expanding the Horizon.**
The cloud is no longer just an option—it's the new normal. As organizations continue to move their data, applications, and services to the cloud, the need for robust cloud security has never been more critical. Cisco's IDS/IPS systems are already built with cloud security in mind, but the future promises even tighter integration with cloud-native technologies. The beauty of cloud security is that it can scale effortlessly to meet the needs of businesses of all sizes. Cisco's future cloud security tools will focus on securing multi-cloud environments, hybrid cloud models, and on-prem infrastructure, offering a holistic security approach. By monitoring and protecting all network traffic in real-time, Cisco ensures that your cloud assets are as secure as your on-prem systems. In a world where data is more fluid and dynamic than ever, Cisco's cloud security will keep your data, applications, and services locked down, no matter where they live. With Cisco IDS/IPS, your network security is not just confined to one location—it's everywhere.

5. **Step 4: Automated Threat Response – The Speed of Light.**
Speed is everything in the fight against cyberattacks. The longer a hacker is in your network, the more damage they can do. That's why automated threat response is a critical feature in the future of Cisco IDS/IPS systems. Instead of waiting for human intervention, Cisco's systems will increasingly respond to threats in real-time, minimizing the impact of attacks. Automated actions like blocking malicious IP addresses, isolating infected machines, or adjusting security policies will happen in milliseconds. This eliminates the lag time between detecting an attack and taking action, ensuring that your defenses are always one step ahead. Think of it as having a fully automated security guard who reacts faster than any human could. The beauty of this automated response is that it doesn't just protect your network—it protects your productivity by minimizing downtime and interruptions. With Cisco's automation, you can be confident that your system is reacting to threats faster than you can say "cybersecurity breach."

6. **Step 5: Threat Hunting – Proactively Searching for Trouble.**
In the future, security will be less about reacting to threats and more about finding them before they find you. Threat hunting is the practice of proactively searching for hidden threats in your network, and Cisco's IDS/IPS solutions are incorporating this feature more than ever. By using real-time monitoring and deep behavioral analysis, Cisco can help security teams identify potential threats before they escalate into full-blown attacks. It's like having a group of digital detectives searching for clues in your network, ensuring that no stone is left unturned. While automated systems can block known threats, threat hunting digs deeper into the unknown, discovering malicious activity that may have evaded the radar. As the threat landscape grows more sophisticated, threat hunting will be a key weapon in the fight against cybercriminals. With Cisco's support, your security team can hunt down and eliminate threats before they get a chance to strike.

7. **Step 6: Next-Generation Firewall Integration – Two Defenders, One Mission.**
The future of network defense isn't about relying on just one tool—it's about integrating multiple layers of security to create a cohesive, unstoppable force. Cisco's IDS/IPS systems will increasingly work in tandem with next-generation firewalls (NGFWs) to provide a unified defense. The next-gen firewall focuses on blocking malicious traffic,

while IDS/IPS systems detect and prevent attacks that have already bypassed the firewall. Together, these two systems form an impenetrable shield around your network. It's like having two bouncers at the door, each with different skills, but working together to keep the party secure. By integrating IDS/IPS with next-gen firewalls, Cisco offers a comprehensive security solution that works at multiple levels to prevent attacks, ensure network integrity, and provide continuous protection.

8. **Step 7: Predictive Analytics – Looking Into the Future of Cybersecurity.**
Imagine being able to predict the future. In cybersecurity, that's precisely what predictive analytics aims to do. Cisco's future IDS/IPS solutions will incorporate predictive analytics to forecast potential threats based on historical data and network behavior. By analyzing trends and anomalies, Cisco can anticipate what might happen next, allowing you to stay ahead of cybercriminals. It's like having a crystal ball that not only tells you what's coming but also provides you with the insight to prepare. Predictive analytics will allow Cisco's IDS/IPS systems to identify emerging attack vectors, predict when and where threats are most likely to occur, and proactively adjust defenses. With predictive analytics, Cisco will not just react to cyberattacks—it will anticipate them.

9. **Step 8: Improved User and Entity Behavior Analytics (UEBA) – Understanding the Who, What, and Why.**
One of the most powerful tools in the future of IDS/IPS is User and Entity Behavior Analytics (UEBA). As the name suggests, UEBA focuses on understanding how users and devices typically behave on your network. By analyzing this baseline of normal activity, Cisco's IDS/IPS system will be able to detect even the most subtle changes in behavior that could indicate a threat. For example, if an employee suddenly accesses sensitive data they have no business looking at, Cisco will flag this as an anomaly, even if there's no obvious sign of malicious intent. This makes it easier to detect insider threats, compromised accounts, and unusual activity that might otherwise go unnoticed. UEBA adds another layer of intelligence to Cisco's security solutions, providing a deeper understanding of network activity and allowing for more targeted, effective defenses.

10. **Step 9: End-to-End Encryption Protection – Securing Data, Inside and Out.**
As encryption becomes a standard for protecting sensitive data, Cisco's IDS/IPS systems will evolve to ensure that encrypted traffic doesn't become a blind spot in your security. Future Cisco solutions will include enhanced capabilities for inspecting encrypted traffic, ensuring that malicious payloads trying to sneak through SSL/TLS connections are detected and blocked. It's like having a security guard who not only watches the front door but also checks the bags of every person trying to sneak in through the side. By securing both encrypted and unencrypted traffic, Cisco ensures that your defenses are airtight, regardless of how data is transmitted. End-to-end encryption protection will become a cornerstone of Cisco's future IDS/IPS systems, providing comprehensive visibility without compromising security or privacy.

11. **Step 10: Cloud-Native IDS/IPS – The Future Is Flexibility.**
The cloud is the future, and Cisco's IDS/IPS solutions are evolving to match. The next frontier in cloud security is the cloud-native IDS/IPS system—built specifically to work

in cloud environments. Traditional on-premises security solutions were designed for static infrastructure, but cloud-native IDS/IPS systems are flexible, scalable, and dynamic, able to adapt to the ever-changing cloud landscape. Cisco will continue to develop cloud-native solutions that seamlessly integrate with public, private, and hybrid cloud environments, ensuring your network stays secure no matter where your data lives. This approach allows businesses to scale their security infrastructure with their cloud adoption, making sure that as their operations grow, their defenses keep pace. Cloud-native IDS/IPS systems will be able to protect workloads, containers, and applications in the cloud, offering comprehensive security that's as flexible as the cloud itself.

12. **Step 11: DDoS Defense 2.0 – The Next Level of Protection.**
DDoS attacks are an ever-present threat, but Cisco is preparing to take DDoS defense to the next level. With the rise of volumetric attacks and more sophisticated techniques, future Cisco IDS/IPS systems will integrate real-time DDoS defense capabilities that can identify and mitigate threats even faster. These enhanced DDoS defenses will not only block malicious traffic but also intelligently distinguish between legitimate and attack traffic, ensuring that your network remains operational during an attack. Think of it as an automated traffic cop who knows when to let through a delivery truck and when to block the protestors. Cisco's next-gen DDoS defense will make sure your network stays functional and responsive, no matter how intense the attack.

13. **Step 12: Distributed Security Architecture – A Unified Approach.**
The future of Cisco IDS/IPS systems will see even more distributed architectures, where security is implemented across every part of your network, from the endpoint to the cloud. By decentralizing security, Cisco ensures that threats are caught and mitigated at the earliest point of entry, preventing lateral movement and reducing the risk of a breach. It's like having security cameras not just at the front door, but at every window and hallway inside the house. This distributed approach will make Cisco's IDS/IPS solutions more resilient and adaptive, able to protect against threats no matter where they originate.

14. **Step 13: Zero Trust Architecture – Trust No One, Verify Everyone.**
Zero trust is quickly becoming the gold standard for network security. The idea behind zero trust is simple: never trust anything, whether it's inside or outside your network— always verify. Cisco's future IDS/IPS solutions will integrate seamlessly with zero trust architectures, ensuring that every user, device, and application is verified before accessing resources. By continuously monitoring traffic and behavior, Cisco ensures that even trusted users and devices aren't allowed to bypass security. Zero trust is an essential part of future network defenses, and Cisco is already leading the way in implementing this philosophy.

15. **Step 14: Privacy and Compliance by Design – Built-In Protection.**
As privacy regulations like GDPR and CCPA become more stringent, future Cisco IDS/IPS systems will be built with privacy and compliance in mind. By incorporating privacy-by-design principles, Cisco ensures that its security systems comply with global regulations while also protecting sensitive data. This means that organizations can achieve robust security while avoiding costly fines for non-compliance. Think of it as a

security guard who not only keeps the bad guys out but also makes sure that all the paperwork is in order. Privacy and compliance won't be an afterthought—they'll be an integral part of Cisco's future IDS/IPS offerings.

16. **Step 15: Behavioral Threat Detection – Understanding the Why.**
Future Cisco IDS/IPS systems will have advanced behavioral threat detection capabilities, enabling them to recognize attacks based not just on technical signatures but also on the context and motivations behind them. By analyzing patterns of behavior and correlating them with known attack methods, Cisco's systems will be able to predict and prevent attacks before they escalate. It's like knowing the criminal's next move before they make it, simply by understanding their behavioral patterns. This advanced threat detection will allow Cisco to stay ahead of emerging threats and protect organizations in ways that traditional systems can't.

17. **Step 16: Multi-Cloud Security – Protecting the New Frontier.**
As more organizations adopt multi-cloud strategies, the complexity of securing cloud environments increases. Cisco's IDS/IPS systems will evolve to offer multi-cloud security, providing seamless protection across public, private, and hybrid cloud environments. By monitoring traffic across all cloud platforms and ensuring that security policies are consistently enforced, Cisco helps businesses secure their cloud assets in a way that's simple, scalable, and comprehensive. With Cisco's multi-cloud solutions, businesses can take full advantage of the flexibility and cost savings of the cloud without sacrificing security.

18. **Step 17: Advanced User and Entity Behavior Analytics (UEBA) – The Smartest Watchdog.**
User and Entity Behavior Analytics (UEBA) will become even more advanced in Cisco's future IDS/IPS systems. By analyzing user and device behavior across the network, Cisco will be able to identify abnormal actions that may indicate malicious activity or compromised accounts. The future of UEBA will provide even more granular insights, detecting threats like insider threats, account takeovers, or privilege escalation attempts. Cisco will be able to track and respond to suspicious behavior faster than ever before, ensuring that threats are contained before they can spread across your network.

19. **Step 18: Threat Intelligence Sharing – Power in Numbers.**
The future of IDS/IPS solutions will be heavily reliant on threat intelligence sharing between organizations, industries, and governments. Cisco's IDS/IPS systems will increasingly integrate with global threat intelligence networks, including Talos, to provide real-time updates and collaborative defense strategies. By sharing information about emerging threats, organizations can strengthen their defenses and work together to combat cybercrime. It's like having a global network of security experts who are all looking out for you, providing you with the latest intelligence to keep your systems secure. Threat intelligence sharing will make future Cisco IDS/IPS systems smarter and more responsive to new threats, ensuring that your defenses are always up to date.

20. **Step 19: Cloud-Native Security Features – Going Beyond Traditional Solutions.**
As organizations continue to embrace cloud-native technologies, Cisco will build even

more cloud-specific features into its IDS/IPS systems. This means that, in addition to protecting traditional on-premises systems, Cisco will provide specialized defenses for cloud workloads, containers, and serverless environments. With more businesses moving to the cloud, securing these platforms will become paramount, and Cisco's cloud-native security will be designed to meet the challenges of this new environment. Cisco's cloud-native IDS/IPS solutions will scale seamlessly with your cloud adoption, ensuring that your security doesn't just grow with your network—it anticipates and protects against future cloud-based threats.

21. **Step 20: AI-Powered Threat Remediation – A Step Ahead of Hackers.**
Future Cisco IDS/IPS systems will leverage AI not just for detection, but for real-time threat remediation. By using AI to predict the impact of potential threats and automatically take defensive actions, Cisco will offer even faster and more precise responses to cyberattacks. Imagine a system that can not only detect an attack but also automatically take the necessary steps to neutralize it—without waiting for human intervention. This AI-powered remediation will enable Cisco's systems to respond to emerging threats faster than hackers can react, keeping your network secure and minimizing downtime.

22. **Step 21: Reducing False Positives – A More Efficient System.**
One of the most frustrating aspects of IDS/IPS systems is the flood of false positives. Future Cisco IDS/IPS systems will use advanced machine learning and behavioral analytics to drastically reduce false alarms. By accurately distinguishing between normal network behavior and suspicious activity, Cisco will ensure that only the most relevant threats are flagged, saving time and effort. It's like having a finely tuned alarm system that only goes off when there's a real threat, allowing your team to focus on what matters most. This will make security operations more efficient, freeing up resources to address higher-priority issues.

23. **Step 22: Integrating with DevOps – Securing the Pipeline.**
With the rise of DevOps practices, Cisco's IDS/IPS solutions will integrate more seamlessly with continuous integration and deployment (CI/CD) pipelines. This will allow security to be embedded directly into the software development lifecycle, ensuring that vulnerabilities are detected and addressed before code is pushed to production. By integrating security into DevOps workflows, Cisco helps organizations build secure applications from the ground up. This shift towards DevSecOps ensures that security isn't an afterthought but an integral part of the development process.

24. **Step 23: Threat Intelligence Correlation – Putting the Pieces Together.**
As the volume and complexity of cyber threats increase, Cisco's IDS/IPS systems will be able to correlate threat data from multiple sources—network traffic, endpoint security, threat intelligence feeds, and more. By correlating data from all these sources, Cisco can provide a comprehensive view of your network's security posture, making it easier to detect and respond to sophisticated attacks. Think of it as connecting the dots between different clues, leading you to a clearer picture of what's happening across your entire

infrastructure. This holistic approach ensures that nothing slips through the cracks, and your response is more targeted and effective.

25. **Step 24: Conclusion – Cisco IDS/IPS: Always Evolving, Always Protecting.**
The future of Cisco IDS/IPS is about more than just responding to threats—it's about anticipating them, evolving with them, and staying ahead of the curve. As the world of cyber threats continues to change, Cisco's IDS/IPS solutions will adapt, incorporating new technologies like machine learning, AI, and cloud-native security. From automated responses to deep integrations with DevOps and cloud platforms, Cisco will continue to innovate, providing organizations with the most powerful, flexible, and intelligent network defense available. With Cisco's IDS/IPS systems, you can rest easy knowing that your network will not only survive the storm—it will thrive, riding the waves of emerging threats and staying one step ahead of the hackers. The future is bright, and Cisco is ready to lead the way.

Chapter 15: Mastering Cisco IDS/IPS – Becoming the Security Maestro Your Network Deserves

1. **Introduction: The Art of Network Defense – A Symphony of Security.**
Welcome to the world of cybersecurity, where every alert, policy, and configuration plays a crucial role in the protection of your network. If managing an IDS/IPS system were like conducting an orchestra, you'd be the maestro, guiding each section to create a harmonious defense against the cacophony of cyber threats. But just like a conductor needs to understand the nuances of each instrument, you need to understand the intricacies of Cisco's IDS/IPS solutions. It's not enough to simply hit the play button on your security system and hope for the best. You have to fine-tune each setting, adjust your thresholds, and synchronize your security policies to ensure that every component works together seamlessly. In this chapter, we're going to explore how you can become the security maestro your network deserves, orchestrating the perfect defense with Cisco's IDS/IPS solutions. Ready to make your network's defenses sing? Let's dive in.

2. **Step 1: The Symphony of Threat Detection – Understanding the Instruments.**
Imagine your network as a grand concert hall, with each device, user, and service acting as an instrument in the orchestra. Cisco's IDS/IPS system is your conductor, ensuring that each component plays its part in keeping out intruders and threats. To become the maestro, you need to understand how each "instrument" works. The network traffic is like the strings section—smooth, fluid, but vulnerable to the wrong note. The firewalls are your percussion—loud, hard-hitting, and blocking anything that doesn't belong. Finally, the IDS/IPS is your brass section—sharp, precise, and always ready to sound the alarm when a threat is detected. Understanding how each element of your security works together is the first step to mastering the Cisco IDS/IPS system.

3. **Step 2: Setting the Tempo – Finding the Right Balance Between Sensitivity and Performance.**
In music, the tempo sets the pace of the entire piece, and the same principle applies to your IDS/IPS system. If your system is too sensitive, you'll get false alarms that flood your inbox like an out-of-tune violin. On the other hand, if it's not sensitive enough, you

risk missing critical threats, like a cello section that's so quiet you can barely hear it. Finding the right tempo means adjusting the thresholds for alerting and detection to ensure that you're catching real threats without overwhelming your team with noise. Cisco allows you to fine-tune these settings, letting you control the rhythm of your security alerts. The key is to find that sweet spot where the system is responsive but not overbearing, alerting you only when it's necessary. This will allow you to keep your network secure while maintaining optimal performance.

4. **Step 3: Conducting Traffic Analysis – Understanding What's Normal.**
Just as a conductor understands the flow of music, you need to understand the flow of traffic within your network. Without a baseline of normal traffic, it's impossible to spot abnormal behavior. Cisco's IDS/IPS system helps you establish this baseline, providing visibility into regular network activity. Once you know what normal looks like, you can easily spot deviations, whether it's an unfamiliar IP address attempting to connect or an unusual spike in traffic. Traffic analysis isn't just about identifying malicious activity—it's about understanding the subtle rhythms of your network so you can quickly pinpoint what's out of place. With Cisco's system, you can monitor traffic patterns and behavior, ensuring that everything runs smoothly and that threats are spotted before they escalate.

5. **Step 4: Fine-Tuning Policies – Composing the Perfect Security Score.**
Your security policies are like the score to a piece of music—each note and phrase is designed to guide your network through the symphony of daily operations. Cisco's IDS/IPS solution allows you to customize these policies to match the unique needs of your network. Are you protecting sensitive data? You might want stricter policies for your financial systems. Are you running a cloud-based infrastructure? You'll need policies that secure your hybrid environment. Fine-tuning your policies involves adjusting settings to ensure that your IDS/IPS system performs in harmony with your network's requirements. Think of it as composing a piece of music—every change you make should serve the greater purpose of securing your network, while also keeping everything running smoothly. With Cisco's granular policy controls, you have the freedom to customize your security to the finest detail.

6. **Step 5: Signature Management – Keep Your Music Current.**
Every piece of music evolves with time—composers update their scores, and orchestras reinterpret old classics. Similarly, your IDS/IPS signatures need to be kept up-to-date to stay effective against the latest threats. Cisco's signature management tools allow you to download the latest updates from Cisco's global threat intelligence network, Talos. By keeping your signatures current, you ensure that your system can identify the newest attack techniques and malware strains. Just like a maestro needs to stay current with new compositions, you need to stay on top of emerging threats. Signature management is essential for maintaining a security system that's always in tune with the evolving landscape of cyber threats. With Cisco's regular updates, your IDS/IPS system will always be ready to face the next big challenge.

7. **Step 6: Alerting – Knowing When to Raise Your Baton.**
In an orchestra, the conductor must know when to raise the baton to cue the musicians,

signaling a shift in the music. Similarly, with your IDS/IPS system, you need to know when to raise the alarm and take action. Cisco's IDS/IPS solution offers customizable alerting, allowing you to set specific thresholds for various types of threats. Whether it's a low-level warning or a critical security breach, you can determine how and when your system notifies you. This fine-tuning is key to making sure you're not overwhelmed by unnecessary alerts while still staying informed about major threats. Think of it as creating a dynamic performance—alerts should be as timely and meaningful as the cues in a live concert, ensuring that you only react to what truly matters.

8. **Step 7: Traffic Filtering – Sifting Through the Noise.**
    In any orchestra, there's always background noise—the sound of chairs scraping, the whisper of audience members. Similarly, your network will always have non-critical traffic that's simply part of the process. Cisco's IDS/IPS solution can help you filter out the noise, ensuring that your system focuses on the traffic that's relevant to your security. With custom traffic filtering, you can block or allow specific types of traffic, ensuring that only legitimate, non-malicious data flows through your network. By eliminating unnecessary alerts and reducing noise, Cisco allows you to focus on the real threats while maintaining a harmonious network environment. This filtering capability ensures that your network defense is more focused, more efficient, and more effective at stopping cybercriminals.

9. **Step 8: Behavioral Analytics – The Art of Recognizing Patterns.**
    Just as a conductor can recognize a musician's style and detect deviations from their usual playing, Cisco's IDS/IPS systems will increasingly use behavioral analytics to spot anomalies within your network. Behavioral analytics works by establishing a profile of normal activity and flagging anything that deviates from it. This helps identify more sophisticated threats, such as insider attacks or advanced persistent threats (APTs), which may not trigger traditional alerts. By using machine learning and behavioral analysis, Cisco's system will get smarter over time, detecting even the most subtle signs of malicious behavior. It's like being able to spot a rogue player in the orchestra just by noticing their playing style has changed. Behavioral analytics gives Cisco's IDS/IPS system the ability to recognize when something isn't quite right, even if it's not immediately obvious.

10. **Step 9: Automated Response – Letting the Music Play On.**
    When you're conducting a live performance, you need to focus on guiding the musicians and ensuring the music flows seamlessly. Similarly, automated response systems in Cisco's IDS/IPS solutions allow you to focus on strategic decisions while the system handles the technical response to threats. Cisco can automatically block malicious IPs, quarantine infected devices, and even update signatures in real-time. This level of automation reduces the time between detection and mitigation, ensuring that your network remains secure even when you're not actively monitoring it. It's like having a team of backup conductors—working tirelessly behind the scenes to ensure that the performance continues without interruptions. With Cisco's automated response, you can rest assured that your system is handling threats without requiring constant human intervention.

11. **Step 10: Threat Intelligence Integration – Expanding Your Orchestra.**
Your orchestra is only as good as the musicians you bring into it. The same is true for your IDS/IPS system—its effectiveness depends on the threat intelligence it uses. Cisco's IDS/IPS solution integrates seamlessly with Cisco's Talos threat intelligence network, ensuring that your defenses are always in tune with the latest global threat data. Talos provides real-time updates on new attack techniques, malware signatures, and vulnerabilities, allowing your system to respond quickly to emerging threats. By feeding this intelligence directly into your IDS/IPS, Cisco ensures that your security system is always prepared for whatever the cybercriminals throw your way. It's like having a constant flow of new sheet music from some of the best musicians in the world, keeping your performance sharp and on point.

12. **Step 11: Customization – Making the Score Your Own.**
Every great conductor puts their own spin on a musical piece, adding their unique interpretation to the score. Similarly, Cisco's IDS/IPS systems allow for a high degree of customization, so you can tailor your security settings to fit the specific needs of your network. Whether you need to fine-tune alerting thresholds, adjust detection methods, or create custom response actions, Cisco gives you the flexibility to make your system work the way you need it to. Think of it as writing your own symphony of security—a performance that's personalized to meet the demands of your unique network environment. With Cisco's customization options, you can make sure that your network is protected in a way that aligns perfectly with your business goals.

13. **Step 12: Continuous Learning – Keeping Your Skills Sharp.**
A conductor is always learning, studying new compositions, and attending rehearsals to improve their craft. Similarly, as a Cisco IDS/IPS maestro, you'll need to continually educate yourself about emerging threats and the latest network security practices. Cisco provides a wealth of training and resources to help you stay ahead of the curve, from online tutorials to certifications and technical documentation. By keeping your skills sharp, you can ensure that you're always prepared for whatever new threats come your way. Learning is a key part of mastering any security system, and Cisco ensures that you have the resources to continuously improve your expertise.

14. **Step 13: Monitoring and Logging – The Conductor's Scoreboard.**
Every great performance needs a scoreboard to track progress, and in cybersecurity, that's your monitoring and logging system. Cisco's IDS/IPS systems offer detailed logging capabilities, tracking every alert, response, and security event that happens across your network. This data is invaluable for analyzing trends, investigating incidents, and refining your security policies. Think of it as your performance review—allowing you to see where your system excels and where improvements might be needed. With Cisco's logging and monitoring tools, you have complete visibility into your network's security, making it easier to fine-tune your defenses and ensure that your security strategy is always on track.

15. **Step 14: Collaboration – Working with Your Security Orchestra.**
No orchestra is made up of just one musician, and no network security system works in

isolation. Cisco's IDS/IPS solutions are designed to integrate seamlessly with other security tools in your environment, from firewalls to SIEM systems to endpoint protection. By collaborating with other security systems, Cisco's IDS/IPS solution ensures that every layer of your defense is working together in harmony. It's like conducting an orchestra where every section—strings, woodwinds, percussion—plays its part to create a beautiful, unified sound. Collaboration is key to creating a robust security posture, and Cisco makes it easy to integrate its IDS/IPS with the rest of your security infrastructure.

16. **Step 15: Incident Response – Taking Action When the Music Stops.**
Every orchestra needs a conductor to guide the musicians during a crisis. Similarly, when a cyberattack occurs, you need to lead your security team through an efficient and effective response. Cisco's IDS/IPS systems provide real-time alerts and automated responses to help you mitigate attacks before they cause significant damage. Whether it's isolating an infected machine, blocking malicious traffic, or updating security policies, Cisco gives you the tools you need to take quick action. Think of it as conducting a swift, coordinated response to a performance hiccup—getting everything back on track without skipping a beat. With Cisco, you can be confident that your network will stay secure, even during the most high-pressure situations.

17. **Step 16: Scalability – Growing Your Orchestra Without Missing a Note.**
As your organization grows, so too will your security needs. Cisco's IDS/IPS solutions are designed to scale with your business, offering the flexibility to protect more devices, users, and services without sacrificing performance. Whether you're expanding to a new office, integrating new cloud platforms, or adding new endpoints, Cisco's systems can easily adapt to accommodate the increase in network complexity. It's like having an orchestra that grows with the talent of its musicians, without losing the quality of the performance. With Cisco's scalable security solutions, you can rest assured that your defenses will keep up with your organization's growth.

18. **Step 17: Threat Intelligence Sharing – A Global Orchestra.**
In the world of cybersecurity, no one is an island. Threat intelligence sharing allows organizations to collaborate, exchanging information about emerging threats and attack techniques. Cisco's IDS/IPS systems integrate with global threat intelligence networks, such as Talos, to provide you with the latest threat data in real-time. This collaborative approach strengthens your defenses, ensuring that you're always one step ahead of cybercriminals. It's like being part of a global orchestra, where every musician is contributing to the collective performance. By sharing knowledge and resources, Cisco ensures that your network security is part of a larger, coordinated effort to combat cybercrime.

19. **Step 18: Adaptability – Responding to Changing Threats.**
Just as a conductor adapts to different musical pieces, you need to adapt to changing threats in the world of cybersecurity. Cisco's IDS/IPS systems are built with adaptability in mind, constantly evolving to meet new attack methods and vulnerabilities. With regular updates from Cisco's Talos threat intelligence network, your system is always

prepared for the latest and greatest threats. As new types of attacks emerge, Cisco's system adjusts, ensuring that your defenses remain sharp and responsive. Adaptability is key to staying ahead in the ever-changing landscape of cybersecurity, and Cisco's IDS/ IPS solutions are always ready for whatever comes next.

20. **Step 19: Testing and Tuning – Perfecting the Performance.**
Even the best orchestras need regular rehearsals to ensure that everything is in tune. Similarly, Cisco's IDS/IPS systems require testing and fine-tuning to ensure that they're performing optimally. Regularly testing your configurations, policies, and response actions helps you identify potential gaps or weaknesses in your defenses. By continuously monitoring performance and adjusting your system, you can ensure that your network remains secure and responsive. Just like musicians refine their playing, you'll need to refine your security practices to ensure that your network is always protected.

21. **Step 20: Staying Ahead of Emerging Threats – The Next Big Composition.**
The world of cybersecurity is always evolving, and staying ahead of emerging threats is like preparing for the next big musical composition. Cisco's IDS/IPS systems are designed to not only react to current threats but to anticipate new attack vectors before they can do damage. By leveraging machine learning, AI, and real-time threat intelligence, Cisco ensures that your defenses are always evolving to meet the needs of the future. It's like preparing for the future performance by studying upcoming music— always staying ahead of the curve. With Cisco's proactive approach, your security strategy will always be one step ahead of the latest threats.

22. **Step 21: Resilience – Bouncing Back from an Attack.**
Even the best orchestras sometimes hit a sour note, but the key is how quickly they recover. In cybersecurity, resilience means quickly recovering from an attack without major disruption to your network. Cisco's IDS/IPS systems are designed to help you bounce back from attacks by isolating infected systems, blocking malicious traffic, and restoring normal network operations. With automated responses and continuous monitoring, Cisco ensures that your network can recover quickly and keep running smoothly, even after a breach. Resilience is an essential quality for any security system, and Cisco's IDS/IPS offers a robust defense that helps your organization stay secure, no matter what.

23. **Step 22: Reporting and Auditing – Keeping Score.**
Just like a conductor keeps track of every note played, you need to keep track of every security event on your network. Cisco's IDS/IPS systems provide comprehensive reporting and auditing features that allow you to analyze trends, review incidents, and assess the effectiveness of your security measures. Whether it's generating compliance reports or investigating suspicious activity, Cisco ensures that you have the data you need to make informed decisions. By keeping a detailed score of your network's security, you can continuously refine your defenses and ensure that you're always prepared for the next performance.

24. **Step 23: Collaboration with IT Teams – A Unified Performance.**
In the world of cybersecurity, you're not conducting a solo performance. To truly master Cisco's IDS/IPS system, you need to collaborate with your IT and security teams. Everyone needs to be on the same page, from network engineers to threat analysts. Cisco's IDS/IPS solutions make it easy to share insights, collaborate on incident response, and work together to strengthen your defenses. By fostering a culture of collaboration, you ensure that your security system is always in sync with your network operations. It's like a conductor working hand-in-hand with the musicians, ensuring that every section plays its part in creating a flawless performance.

25. **Step 24: Conclusion – Becoming the Maestro of Your Network Security.**
By mastering Cisco's IDS/IPS solutions, you can become the security maestro your network deserves. You'll be able to conduct your security strategies with precision, adapting to the changing landscape of cyber threats and keeping your defenses in harmony. From traffic analysis to automated responses, from policy tuning to threat intelligence, Cisco's IDS/IPS systems provide you with the tools you need to protect your network from every angle. As the cyber threat landscape continues to evolve, Cisco's systems will evolve with it, ensuring that your defenses remain strong and adaptive. With Cisco, you're not just reacting to attacks—you're orchestrating a powerful defense that's always ready for the next wave. So, step up to the podium, grab your baton, and start conducting your network security symphony. Your network deserves it.

www.ingramcontent.com/pod-product-compliance
Lightning Source LLC
LaVergne TN
LVHW081531050326
832903LV00025B/1736